My Dear Ak'i, Please Don't Be Upset

by Faisu Mukunana

Translator: Yao-Chung Tsao

Editor: Cort Smith

2021

伐依絲・牟固那那

武 香 梅

"This is a book of profound memories of the past. Seen through the lens of a female Tsou tribal member of Taiwan, Faisʉ's writing style flows fluently in describing the scenes of aboriginal lives and the changes that occurred throughout the 1950s and 1960s. Her writing is never servile nor overbearing but truthful and vivid. Drawing upon her own experiences growing up in the tribal community, she brings to life events and scenery of her homeland, the customs of her people, and offers colorful descriptions of the manual labor that was necessary for their survival. The result is a compelling mosaic of daily life.

"Remote in time and distance (the author currently lives in Taipei), Faisʉ cherishes her recollections of the Tsou's land and songs and folklore, and recounts with emotion the forever-gone time and life of her native land. Fortunately for future generations, she leaves a path for them to explore this past, and honor and treasure the spirit of their ancestors along the way."

Mr. Sun Ta-chuan (Paelabang Danapan), Scholar, a Puyuma tribe member of Taiwan.

"Faisʉ, in her opening story bearing the same title as the book, talks to her grandfather at his grave. Through this spiritual communication, Faisu allows us an emotional and intimate glimpse into the lives of the native Tsou people of Taiwan, thus drawing us into the interesting anthropological lore contained in the chapters that follow. As a scholar familiar with California (USA) native American traditions, I am struck by the similarities of Tsou spiritual beliefs and practices with those of many native Americans."

"In her talk with her Ak'i (grandfather), Faisʉ expresses guilt that she and her family 'forgot' about him for 51 years, never sweeping or visiting his grave. She mentions to him that she realizes it had not been Tsou custom in the past to attend to the dead so devotedly and she seems to wonder about it, to the extent of apologizing to her Ak'i for seeming so 'uncaring.' Indeed, the reader may have those same thoughts. As a scholar of native American spiritual practices, I see parallels that may provide some explanation, both for the general reader and for other scholars on these subjects. For example, the Chumash of Southern California traditionally 'forgot' about the newly dead in order to help their dead break from the emotional ties to their past life and physical pleasures. In Chumash tradition, Scorpion Woman assists souls, toward the end of their journey on the 'path of the dead,' by stinging them so they will forget the life they just left and be content while waiting in the celestial paradise to be reborn. Perhaps, like the Chumash, the Tsou deliberately ignored their dead, thus assisting them to continue on the 'path of the dead' toward reincarnation, when their family might see them again. This is a topic that would be fascinating to learn more about from the Tsou people. I enjoyed the book very much."
Dr. John Anderson, Scholar in Native American History.

"I'm inspired by the incredible vision, perseverance and cooperation within the family and beyond expressed with precise details and analogies. I can imagine the deep sense of purpose, effort, and emotion of each person. Her writing is a wonderful mix of memory, love, cultural anthropology, and insight wrapped up in great storytelling. I'm so glad she got windows in her family's new house because she brings light to so many."
Dr. Pamela Burke, Educator

"Paicu'e Muknana, the author, changed her first name to Faisu later in her adult life, a name that is traditionally used by the Tsou people to show respect for a senior female tribal member. Muknana is her family name; its pronunciation sounds close to 武 (/wu/) in Mandarin, therefore 武 (Wu) is used as her family name in the Han community. The Muknana clan belongs to a much larger Yasiungu clan which is a branch of Tfuya sub-tribe. Faisu grew up in a remote, tribal hillside village called Yayovea of Lalauya. This book is based on her memories of the traditional Tsou life experiences growing up in Lalauya.

"Due to her marriage at an early age with a man originally from Mainland China, and also because, early in her life, she left the familiar tribal village and moved to a community that is dominated by the Mandarin language and Han culture, she has become an exquisite bilingual writer fluent in the Tsou language and proficient in Mandarin writing. With her sophisticated writing skills (concise, precise, fluent, and meticulous), she portrays various facets of the Tsou's centuries-old way of life prior to 1970s and before the drastic modernization and urbanization that impacted them. Their traditional life used to be rustic and unique, simple and modest. I, a Tsou member of a later generation from the same tribal village as Faisu's, am deeply inspired by her writings, always lively and vivid, that have engaged readers like me. The probable reason why she used *My Dear Ak'i, Please Don't Be Upset* as the book title is because she is married to a Han man, not a Taiwanese Han but a Han from Mainland China across the Taiwan Strait. Consequently, she finds herself existing in between the Tsou and Han cultures, and she seems to want to convey some messages to her grandpa, to current and future Tsou generations, to the Han Taiwanese, and to the relatively recent Chinese immigrants (and their offspring) who fled from China to Taiwan after the Second World War. Sharing her memories of growing up in what she considered a pristine and culturally rich environment, may provide a means for helping lessen tensions that have been around for a long time between the aboriginal and the Han, between Taiwanese and recent Chinese immigrants, and among the Taiwanese who have been struggling over their national identity—so that without anger they can calmly engage in constructive dialogue with respect and mutual understanding."

Dr. tibusungu 'e vayayana (Ming-huey Wang), Professor, a Tsou tribe member of Taiwan

Table of Contents

Author's Comments for English Readers

First, as a devoted Christian converted at a young age, I thank the almighty God who has sent me two angels—my gentlemen supporters—Professor Yao-Chung Tsao and Mr. Cort Smith, to translate my modest first book, *My Dear Ak'i, Please Don't Be Upset,* into English. They asked me to write a note for this English edition. On the one hand, I am deeply indebted to their tremendous endeavor in translating the book, while at the same time, I am truly nervous and somewhat uneasy to have my humble self and the book exposed to the readers of the unfamiliar English world. I would be very happy of course if you read this book. My blessing to you, my dearest reader! Last, I'd like to dedicate this book to my beloved Tsou tribal members.

Faisʉ Mʉkʉnana

Translator's Notes

Around 2008, Ms. Hsin-I Tseng introduced me to Faisʉ Mʉkʉnana and to her book, published in 2003, *My Dear Ak'i, Please Don't Be Upset.* I was fascinated by the short stories it contains regarding her experiences growing up and as an adult in the Tsou community in Taiwan. As a skillful storyteller, her tales are engaging, subtle, and always interesting; and there are stories within stories. Within these pages one can sense the various issues confronting Taiwan today. They affect indigenous Tsou people in particular and all of the people in general, and are of social, cultural, racial, psychological, and political significance. Remarkably, she conveys all this in a gentle and humorous way. As a human cognition psychologist by training, I too am interested in and sensitive to these issues.

In early 2017, I began to translate the book into English. In the process, I have encountered several challenging issues. First and foremost, how could my efforts help future English readers better understand, and benefit from, the stories of a minority culture in a different time? I decided to provide an ample number of footnotes, to both support and reinforce the text. Given that Faisʉ and I were born of the same year, we both have lived under two regimes (Japan and Republic of China). We both have witnessed and confronted the political, social, cultural, and economic changes and challenges that have occurred over the last seventy-some years in Taiwan. In this regard, the footnotes are to more fully share our mutual experiences with you, our English reader.

During the translation process, I was fortunate to be able to correspond with Faisu from time to time to ensure my proper understanding of the original text as well as its context. I am indebted to Mr. Cort Smith for his professional editing expertise, and for providing feedback and suggestions regarding my translation. He and I have held numerous meetings to deliberate over details, big and small. I am truly grateful to him; our work together has formed the bond of our friendship. In her role as project manager and much more, Ms. Liu Ya-Mei (the daughter of the author) has actively explored a variety of publication-related resources. Due to this effort, Ms. C. J. Anderson-Wu was brought on board to provide feedback for the translation format, to help investigate publication venues, to support the fundraising process, and finally, to coordinate various aspects of the publication. And she in turn connected us with Ms. Lin Yi-Miao, the chief editor of Taiwan Indigenous Voice Publishing House which publishes this book.

Finally, a grant from the National Culture and Arts Foundation (國藝會) of Taiwan has helped make publication possible. We greatly value their support.

Yao-Chung Tsao

1. Mythology and Ancestors

阿里山 達邦 戰祭
心儀 171. 2002

My Dear Ak'i, Please Don't Be Upset [1]

My dear Ak'i (grandpa), you have been here for more than 50 years; to be exact, 51 years.[2] One of your descendants, your eldest son who was also my *amo* (father), followed you twenty-some years ago, and so did several of my *amoconi* (uncles). Right now, only the fourth *amoconi* is still alive, but he is 78 years of age. Throughout this long period of time, I, Paiz,[3,4] your granddaughter, remember that only during the first few years after you passed away did we often think about you and come here to visit. After that, we nearly forgot all about you. We let you stay here all alone in this bamboo forest, which is damp and deprived of sunlight. My dear Ak'i, please don't be upset.

Before the arrival of the Tomb Sweeping Day this year,[5] my younger sister and I returned to our old family house, where we grew up, to sweep the nearby tombs of our *amo* and *ino* (mother). My dear Ak'i,

---

1. *Author's note: This article received the 2nd place award at the Second Aboriginal Essay Writing Competition sponsored by the Chung Hwa Motor Company, Year 2000.*

(The following notes in this book are all by the translator, unless otherwise stated.)

2. *This article was written in the year 2000.*

3. *In the Tsou's language, a person's name appears before a pronoun; e.g., "Paiz, I." However, in this English edition, the reverse format is used in order to follow the English style.*

4. *In 2007, she changed her name to Faisu Mukunana. Paiz means "lovely and young"—a name deemed more suitable for teenage girls. Her Mandarin Chinese name is Shiang-Mei Wu, 武香梅.*

5. *The Tomb Sweeping Day is on April 5th each year.*

as you know, the customs of Tomb Sweeping Day and associated tomb sweeping ceremonials were not in our tradition. We Tsou people used to treat the matters of life and death as an inherent part of Great Mother Nature, and our way of living followed Her seasons in the manner of farmers planting specific crops at certain times of year. The Christian Bible describes death as "Ashes to ashes, dust to dust." The Tsou people seem to hold a very similar attitude. Therefore, our longings for the ancestors are all but formality, and we tend to forget about our deceased elders unless we really try hard to remember them.

During the time the Tsou still lived in thatch or bamboo houses,[6] when a family member passed away (we called it "the person is going bad") and while the body was still warm, it would be posed in such a way that it would appear to be sitting with the knees bent and the arms crossed over the chest. A wood stick was used to ensure the desired posture. We all knew that the body, while resembling a fetus inside a mother's womb, instead was really a person in Mother Nature's embrace. When it was time for the burial, a hole at the central area of the family house was dug, the deceased family member was lowered into it, and the hole was then covered with dirt. Above it, a wood pile was made and then lit.

I have no idea how far back this memorial tradition started, and you, the elderly Ak'i, may not know either. Of course, there were other ceremonial activities performed at the same time. Within five days of the burial, for example, all family members were forbidden to work or

---

6. *The Tsou's housing style began to change to modern day structures under Japan's influence in the early 20th century—a trend that continued into the Republic of China's rule beginning in 1945.*

travel very far, to show respect to the dead; at night, family members slept on a mat next to the fire in order to comfort the dead. Once the ground by the house was full with corpses, the living family moved on to a new site, leaving the house and bodies behind, allowing the trees and grass to grow back.

Historically, the Tsou people had no use for tombstones, since human remains were gradually returned to nature and the precious spirit to the eternal resting place, the Pagoda Mountains, located southwest of the present day Alishan Tourist Area. For that reason, the deceased would be buried facing the Pagoda Mountains. The departed who had performed good deeds in life would go to Big Pagoda Mountain, while the ones who hadn't behaved very well went straight to Small Pagoda Mountain.

My dear Ak'i, you also know that we Tsou don't have a writing system to record various events that have happened, therefore, I, Paiz, often regret and sigh that we cannot pass on our beautiful culture

Pagoda Mountains. The mountain in the front is the Big Pagoda Mountain and the one in the back is the Small Pagoda Mountain.

and historical events, clearly and truthfully, to our future generations. It is like a chef who has plenty of great ingredients but no available fire or fuel, and must therefore borrow from the neighbors in order to cook. Alas, food would taste different even prepared with the same ingredients and cooking procedures if other kinds of fuel were used. Similarly, borrowing a writing system from another culture to record the Tsou's history and events somehow gives me that feeling as well. It makes me think that some special, subtle flavor is missing, one that only we Tsou could smell and tell the difference. With no proper writing system, ancestors would be forgotten in three to four generations, unless they were so distinguished that their legacies were worthy of being orally told and retold among family and friends throughout the ages.

The previous so-called "country" you knew about, my dear Ak'i,[7] prohibited our burial tradition. They wanted us to follow their procedure of putting the dead body in a wooden box, called a casket, and burying it. Dear Ak'i, I remember this was also the way you were buried here. The grave was surrounded by stones, and plants of red stems and leaves were grown on the grave. From the time I was a small child, I have called the plant "dead people plant," because I have seen it on almost every grave. So whenever I see the plant growing somewhere, I just assume the ground must have been a burial site.

A wooden grave sign was erected after your burial was completed, Ak'i. But within a very few years the wooden sign had decayed. The result of that natural occurrence, along with our, your descendants',

---

7. *Here the author refers to Japan. This is a defiant expression she uses to suggest that Japan was a country from "outside" and therefore not the Tsou's true country.*

negligence left us feeling embarrassed that we couldn't find your grave; we even swept the wrong one the last time we came out here. To make matters worse, our fourth *amoconi* (uncle) forgot the exact location of your grave, and not seeing anywhere a tombstone with your name upon it, complained to my father, a stone cutter, and asked him why he had never cut one for you. But Amoconi should have known that, since we Tsou never had such a thing called a tombstone, it was pointless to go looking for one, let alone criticize my father for not making one! My *amo* probably had never thought that things would have changed so much over the next generations and that your descendants would learn the good tradition of the *putu* (the Han people) to remember their ancestors. Anyway, that's why no tombstone was ever erected for you, Ak'i.

****

Dear Ak'i, do you remember that before you passed away, the previous so-called "country" was replaced by the present "country?"[8] While these outside countries have nothing to do with our Tsou traditions and history, they like to count us among their territories. Japan called us "Royal Citizens." They wanted us to speak their language, and dress the way they dressed. As a result, it's hard to find any Tsou women of our generation who can weave Tsou's fabric. I haven't even seen a traditional Tsou weaving machine!

Years ago, the Republic of China, the present day "country," want-

---

8. *The author refers to the Republic of China, which took over the control of Taiwan from Japan in 1945. This is a defiant expression the author uses to say that the Republic of China is a country from the "outside," not the "inside," or the Tsou's true country.*

ed us Tsou to learn how to live a "civilized material life," and towards that end created a slogan, "The Movement of Improving Indigenous People's Lives." This movement, enforced for a few years, promoted various competitions among the Tsou. They began at the lowest competition level, or unit, called *lin* (鄰), which means neighborhood; next was the village or *tsun* (村) level, followed by the district level (鄉), and, finally, the province level (省). It would have taken a tremendous amount of time, hard work, and financial resources for a busy farming family to be able to hang certificates of merit on the walls of their house for winning all these competitions!

Thanks to this "movement," in order to keep up with the Joneses even families short on financial resources felt they had to overhaul their homes. Ak'i, after you passed away, my *amo* followed suit. He replaced the bamboo house you knew so well, the one made of limestone cement. He also spent money during the period of financial hardship to purchase household appliances that would comply with the competition rules. Dear Ak'i, before that, didn't we only use utensils that were made of wood, bamboo, or rattan? To impress the competition judges, my *amo* purchased two shiny face-washing basins and kitchen utensils made of aluminum. Sure, they did look more beautiful than the old kind. Regrettably, the utensils Amo made were no longer in use by that time, so we never learned how to make them. A lot of skills were lost, Ak'i, and I am saddened. For us it is too late to begin cherishing our ancestors' knowledge and skills and heritage— we can yearn for them, but they are gone and we cannot bring them back.

During this period we were told by the abrupt and uncompromising authorities that we should learn to speak the "national language"[9] used by the so-called "country." Because of that, I, your granddaughter, while not a particularly good student of the primary school, was humiliated several times when I inadvertently spoke the Tsou language that I had learned since I was in Ino's womb. Anyone caught speaking in their native tongue would have to wear for a full day a wooden plate on their chest with the words "rule violation." Some senior, naughty fellow students would say right to my face: "How stupid you are, still speaking the aboriginal language!" As innocent as I was, I only felt humiliated and puzzled. Why was it wrong to speak Ino's language? I dared not play in the school yard even though I was fond of playing outdoors. Besides, how could I, slender and small, play when wearing a big wooden plate on my chest? My dear Ak'i, I don't think you ever experienced these kinds of things! Did you?

Since the time our lives were turned upside down by these two major powers—first Japan and then the Republic of China—we indigenous Tsou have lost much in terms of our culture and traditions. Well, decades have passed. In order to live in today's world, your descendants have gradually left behind most Tsou traditions and adopted "modern" ways of work and life; many have even left our homeland to make their living elsewhere. I have married a *putunoapihana* (a Han person from the other side of the Taiwan Strait). Marrying a *putunoapihana* has been a very common occurrence among your grandchildren and great-grandchildren. So I hope you, my dear Ak'i, will not be upset by the fact that I married one. These days, your descendants have learned about sweeping graves on the Tomb Sweeping Day, in memory

---

9. *The author refers to Mandarin Chinese, the official and national language of the Republic of China.*

of the ancestors and to receive their blessings. This is something good that we have learned from the *putu*.

While we have remembered to sweep our parents' graves, alas, we have forgotten to sweep yours! It is not that we haven't thought of you during the many decades we haven't seen you. But, rather, we have thought of you and grandma and your sons—our father and uncles— who during the period of time when there were few tools to cultivate rice fields in the stony, steep mountains, did so with callused feet and hands all while opening up lands in the forests on both sides of the Yayoveya Mountain valley. This initiative showed your far-sighted vision, as these areas proved rich in water resources.

Your approach to farming was clearly driven by something I had first noticed when I was a small child, namely that both sides of the mountain valley contained a greater variety of vegetation than that on our neighbors' lands. You had also cultivated a lot of rice fields on the flat land, as well as on the mountain slopes. Though your land was divided by your five sons, each of them with a modest share, every bit of it was the result of your blood and sweat. These things always make me think of you, Ak'i, and always make me grateful for you in my heart. When your descendants considered selling their shares of the land, I even stopped them, and told them this land was the result of your hard work clearing thorny shrubs and weeds, and that therefore we must cherish it. Although most of the land is steep hills, still, it is the land that Tsou people can count on and come home to after they are exhausted from living in a foreign land.

I, Paiz, remember this: Before I attended the primary school, one day my parents were working far away and couldn't come home for lunch. You, Ak'i, cooked the lunch for my elder brother, me, and other grandchildren. I remember very well that your hair was gray, and your back could not be held upright due to decades of overwork and over-exhaustion. (This was my image of you, not the tall, handsome, young man remembered by the village elders.) At the lunch, you let my brother and me share the piece of chicken that was specially put aside for you by my father, your eldest son. If this had been witnessed by my *amo*, he would have scorned us for our lack of respect. During the years when it was a rare occasion to slaughter a chicken, everyone in the family was given the same amount. But Amo would offer you two chicken drums.

You of course will recall, my dear Ak'i, that according to traditional Tsou etiquette, when fish or meat was served, each family member received an equal portion of it. Children were given portions equal to those of the adults because kids needed nutrition in order to grow; the elderly received more out of respect. However, since old age had taken away most of your teeth, you couldn't eat as fast as we youngsters could, gobbling food like hungry ghosts while you had to consume each delicacy very slowly. We would stare at your chicken drums at meal time, and use our memory of what chicken meat smelled like—imaginary flavor to go along with rice! You understood what your grandchildren had in mind, but you would never offer us your chicken drums in the presence of Amo, for fear of him being angry with us; he respected you very much. Instead, you waited until Amo wasn't around to show your love and care for us.

I remember this also. When I was a small child, I liked to watch you sleeping on your bamboo bed, seeing your eyes closed, mouth closed, sleeping with very regular, smooth breathing. When you breathed out, the air would push out your lips with sounds of *"brrr."* How fascinating this was!

I forget exactly to what special occasion our entire family were invited in order to celebrate at my eldest aunt's, but it was rather hilarious. Before we left the house, I saw in your front chest pocket what you had prepared for yourself: some dried tobacco leaves you had grown and dried, a pipe you made out of a bamboo root, and a lighter. In addition, you had something wrapped in dried banana leaf. It smelled very fragrant, a mixed sauce of salt, pepper powder, and pea-nut powder. This was a special sauce you used when you were having a meal, but we were always afraid to try it. We realized later that the sauce made by other tribal people was not strong enough for you, Ak'i, and that you needed to bring your own!

Your granddaughter, I, Paiz, who wasn't very sharp, could only remember this much about you when you passed away, though I was already in the second grade. My dear Ak'i, please don't be mad at me.

****

Why do I come here today to disturb your peace, after not having come to visit you for so many decades? My dear Ak'i, it is because someone named Iusungu wants to see you, a great-grandson of yours, the eldest grandson of my youngest uncle. He is 19 years old, and has lived since he was a small boy with his parents in a Han community on the flat plain.[10] A college student in Taipei when I saw him on February

---

10. *Most Taiwanese aborigines live in the mountains and are called "Mountain People," and most Han people live on the flatlands and are called "Plains People."*

15th of this year,[11] he was no longer the shy middle-schooler back when we first met at the Mayasvi (Tsou War Festival) in our hometown of Tfuya (特富野). He had borrowed a red Tsou outfit from someone to give the impression that he was a Tsou warrior. In my mind, I was thinking, "What a child! He thinks putting on red clothes would make him a Tsou warrior?" At Tfuya, he told me he would find time to ask me about the Mʉkʉnana family heritage, the family that had resided in the valley of Yayoveya. (Mʉkʉnana is our family name in the Tsou language; it was later changed to Wu [武] by the current "country.")

Not long after that, this kid actually came to my house. He told me that he didn't speak the Tsou language because he had lived outside the Tsou community since he was a small child, and that his father didn't want him to learn Tsou, lest he be looked down upon by his classmates. A case in point: My aunt-in-law, who married your youngest son (that is, my youngest uncle) after you passed away, didn't receive a formal education; therefore, she couldn't speak the language of the present "country." However, in order to communicate with her grandchildren, who could not speak our Tsou mother tongue, she tried her best to learn to speak Mandarin. But she spoke the language so poorly that her grandchildren laughed at her. This situation is common among most of your children and grandchildren. If you were still alive today, you wouldn't be able to communicate with your own grandchildren! And that is why I ask, my dear Ak'i, please don't be upset.

After this boy, Iusunga, attended college, and maybe because he had finally grown up, he began to wonder about his heritage—his family origin and background, his upbringing. He was curious about the

---

11. *The year 2000.*

Tsou's history, culture, and traditions. He said he seemed to have lost a lot of knowledge that he should have possessed, and thus is vexed. He wants to go back and start over again. He asked me, "Is it too late?" My reply: "As long as there is a beginning, it would never be too late."

I was extremely embarrassed by your great-grandson when he asked me this: "Where is my great-grandfather, your *ak'i*? Why have I never seen his grave?" This question really made me speechless. I didn't have an answer for it, because no one had ever asked such a question. In response, I told him about our tradition of burial, and our views regarding life and death and so on. But he was dissatisfied by my answers, as though I were giving him the runaround. His world view and very way of thinking about and understanding things were vastly different from those of the Tsou. He insistently asked me: "How come the great-grandpa doesn't have a grave? How come no one thinks about him?" No wonder he is confused; our negligence has made it impossible for him to understand.

My dear Ak'i, you should be very happy today, because among your many descendants finally one of them thinks of you, and wants to find you! I promised him, this boy, Iusunga, that I would look for your grave, that memories provide me some notion of where it may be. Several years after you passed away, my *amo* and I had often presented you with a bowl of cooked rice, and burned incense for you. The custom of presenting rice and burning incense wasn't our Tsou's tradition; we learned it from the previous "country." Our Tsou saying is: "Human spirit goes to where spirit belongs, where there is food for the spirits. They shouldn't share food with the living."

After having been moved out of the house for more than 30 years—

from the time that I was married—I was actually concerned whether I could find your grave, knowing it didn't have a tombstone. The last time we three sisters came home, we intended to ask our fourth uncle, who was still in very good health, about your grave's whereabouts. We were unable to find him, however, mainly because we hadn't tried to inform him of our intent ahead of time. So we decided to search for your grave ourselves.

We used the scythe I bought in northern Taiwan, picking the shortest path across a steep slope full of bamboo plants and overgrown grass. I was leading the way, and cleared a path. This reminded me of a Tsou youth who once stated without exaggeration: "We the Tsou people don't need to bend when we clear grass." The young man meant that since the land reserved for the Tsou tribe was mostly steep rocky hills (and difficult to cultivate), one could clear the grass ahead by standing up rather than bending down. For example, from where I was standing that time, the grass I cut moving forward was at about my eye level. Sometimes I even had to raise my head to cut it!

Finally, we reached an area that was somewhat flat and saw "dead people plants" and piles of stones. I convinced myself that this place ought to be your grave. My sisters and I laboriously removed the weeds and swept the area clean, a very important task. But that evening, when a cousin of our second uncle returned from a training workshop, he told us that we had gone to a totally wrong location. When asked where it should be, he said he didn't know, because he had been away from home for many years. He advised us to ask Mr. Wu, who lived in Pcopcoknʉ.[12]

---

12. *Present day Zu-Giaw (*竹腳*).*

I have known Mr. Wu since childhood. We lived in the same neighborhood district, and he had been the captain of our young student procession in the walk to and back from school.[13] We school kids lined up in one column early in the morning at a specific time, and it was up to Mr. Wu to lead our column and maintain order throughout the round trip, which took many hours in total.

In order to find you, the next day we left the house not much later than five o'clock, and headed to Mr. Wu's place. When we arrived, to our embarrassment, the whole family was still asleep. As I recall, Mr. Wu and his parents were hard-working people. They often had the house in order before dawn, and kept it neat and orderly all day long. Daily tasks included feeding the livestock, and cleaning the inside and outside of the house. After their breakfast, at daybreak, adults went to the mountains to work and kids went to school to study.

But today, at almost six o'clock, all was quiet. After calling them a few times, finally someone answered the door. What happened? Well, Mr. Wu wasn't young anymore. He had eye problems, and he couldn't work as hard as he used to. Also, since every family owned some sort of transportation vehicle nowadays, there was no need to get up early in the morning to walk to some mountain top or valley, oftentimes a time-consuming distance away, which they had to do previously. I apologized repeatedly to Mr. Wu's family for disturbing them at such an early hour. To my surprise, however, they seemed pleased. In this neighborhood district the number of people in my age group was gradually shrinking, not to mention that people also had spread out geo-

---

13. *There were no school buses then in Taiwan, and they are rare throughout the country even today.*

graphically; it was no longer easy for them to meet with one another. For these reasons—and maybe others—Mr. and Mrs. Wu appeared to be very, very delighted we were there.

I explained to Mr. Wu the reason for our visit. He said that even though he didn't remember exactly which grave was yours, Ak'i, he still enthusiastically led my younger sister and me in search of it. He said that when you were buried, he was already in the fifth grade. He vaguely remembered squatting on a large rock covered by moss, due to lack of sunshine, watching adults dig a hole in the ground and lower you into it. After so many years, though, it was clear that since there were several unmarked graves circled by rocks, there was no way Mr. Wu could be certain which one was yours.

Since we couldn't find your grave that day, I returned home disappointed but determined to find it in the future, so that I, Paiz, would have an answer for your persistent and devoted descendant, Iusunga.

After I returned to Northern Taiwan, a cousin I hadn't visited during the last search heard about my desire to find your grave, and called me. She remembered clearly where your grave was because it's next to her mother's. Thank God! But my cousin had just returned from visiting that burial area and had no plan to go back there again until after the Tomb Sweeping Festival.

Dear Ak'i, let me pause here to tell you about this past Tomb Sweeping Festival. I joined for the first time with your grandson-in-law, a *putunoapihana*, to help sweep his ancestors' graves in his hometown, thousands of kilometers away in Sichuan, China (中國四川). The organization, the Liu Kinship Association for Tomb Sweeping Festival (劉氏宗

親清明會),[14] was recently reactivated after decades of interruption due to government policies.[15]

This trip was an eye-opening experience for your granddaughter, me, Paiz. On the one hand it made me admire how much the Liu descendants remembered and honored their ancestors, while on the other it made me ashamed that I couldn't even find my grandpa's grave.

At nine o'clock in the morning on the day of Tomb Sweeping Festival, the various Lius gathered at one place. When descendants of the branches of the family trees had all arrived, they began the grandiose procession, striking cymbals and drums, toward the graves of their ancestors. These forbears, who arrived at Sichuan and settled there, went as far back as ten or more generations. Once they arrived at the grave sites, they bowed to the graves. Then descendants of each family tree branch proceeded to sweep the graves of their respective ancestors, who represented many generations. By noon, having finished, they had lunch together, using a total of 36 dinner tables. (I was told there were 60 tables several years ago. In general, there were usually ten to 12 persons per table.) The descendants of various family branches took this opportunity to get to know each other, and to network. Some of them even brought out their family genealogy books to show that they were authentic descendants of the Liu family and could trace their history back as far as 2,000 years ago. I was really amazed,

---

14. *Liu is her husband's family name.*

15. *For 40 years, China experienced a major upheaval resulting in the discounting and eradication of many old Chinese traditions. The movement from May 6, 1966 to October 6, 1976, called the Chinese Cultural Revolution, was orchestrated by Mao Zedong to attack and harass members of China's elderly and intellectual population. The impact would be felt for decades.*

and greatly admired them.

Looking at how the relatives on my husband's side so profoundly honored and remembered their ancestors, I was truly mortified and ashamed to admit to myself that I couldn't even find your grave. How could I face the collective spirits of the Tsou ancestors? How could I explain it to them? Would it be satisfactory to just say it was our, the Tsou's, tradition? Would it be enough to simply say "I am embarrassed?" No.

And that's why I came back here today. Leading the way was my cousin—whose mother's grave, it turned out, was next to yours, Ak'i. We had found it! A mixed feeling of excitement and sadness occupies my heart. Finally, after 51 years, we meet again.

The Tsou tribe is a patriarchal society, yet your great-grandson, Iusungu, who has been searching for you, couldn't be here. As you know, a woman becomes an outsider of the family where she was born and raised, and becomes a family member of her husband's. Well, since my cousin and I are married, we needed to have a male family member with us to witness what we have done today. Therefore, we have with us Avai, the eldest son of my eldest brother. My dear Ak'i, he should learn much more about you.

It hasn't been easy to find your grave; all we can do today is some weeding, and clear the surrounding area. Regarding grave repair: This is a major endeavor, and should involve your descendants of the Mukʉnana family in the Yayoveya Valley. A descendant of yours even suggested that we should also create a family genealogy book of the Mukʉnana family in the valley of Yayoveya. I think this is a rather good idea; we should.

Dear Ak'i, we know your name in Tsou language was Voyu Mʉkʉnana. However, we don't know what names you were given by the previous "country" and the current "country." In order to repair your grave, and to create the family genealogy book of the Mʉkʉnana family in the valley of Yayoveya, we need to know that information. Therefore, I applied for the original household documents issued by the previous and the current "countries," and learned that the previous "country" gave you a Japanese name of Mukino Kinsuke (向野金助); Mukino (向野) was the last name, Kinsuke (金助) the first. And the current "country" gave you the name of Wu Tsumin (武助明); Wu (武) was the last name, Tsumin (助明) the first.

Now comes the question: Which name should be used on your gravestone and in our family genealogy book? If we use the names given by the so-called "countries," then how would your Tsou spirit and physical characteristics be manifested? As you are aware, if a foreign name is assigned to a person, then that spirit and characteristics are lost in the name. Only a Tsou name will work! But if we use your name in the Tsou language—alas, it was not registered in the governmental documents—it could cause as much confusion for future descendants as it has already caused me, and it would require of them as much work to properly understand it as it already has of me!

In search of you, your granddaughter Paiz's heart was full of excitement, but now, suddenly, it is puzzled. Since we left you in the ground, you've spent 51 lonely years there. Then we came back here, unexpectedly, to not just disturb you but, even worse, to annoy you with all of the hustle, bustle, and fracas of this secular world. All I can do is to say to you: "Dear Ak'i, please do not be *too* upset."

Fragrant Sticky Rice — A Mythological Story From the Tsou[16]

It was a long, long time ago, when a young man—the father of two lovely kids—hiked deep into the mountains to find food for his family. Having heard there was a lot of *ta'eucu*, a kind of tasty tendril-like vine[17], and told where to go, off he went armed with a basket, a small hoe, and a scythe.

Although he was physically fit, he felt tired and was short of breath due to the long and difficult mountain trails. He stuck his neck out to scan far ahead, hoping to get there as soon as possible. When there was no trail to walk on, he swung his scythe to clear the shrub. Finally, he arrived at the spot where there was a lot of *ta'eucu*.

He began to dig. He dug up many *ta'eucu* tubers, and each and every one was huge. He put them in the basket, so many that in no time the basket was almost full. He thought, just a couple more before

---

16. Author's note: "This was the fairy tale about how the fragrant sticky rice was introduced to the Tsou people. I remember, when I was a child, there weren't enough irrigated rice paddy fields to grow sufficient rice for the family. So we also grew early crops of rice on the dried land, including the fragrant sticky rice which was required for religious ceremony purposes. The seed head of each fragrant sticky rice carries a similar structure to that of wheat at the end of a grain. When the husk of a sticky rice grain is opened, its fragrance will emerge immediately. The scent becomes even stronger when steamed. Every time when I reflect on it, I become immersed in this wonderful fragrance. How memorable it is."

17. This is the Asian mountain yam, whose tuber is edible.

he headed home. "Oh my, what a huge tuber!" he proclaimed, picking up another. He continued digging, and digging; there seemed no end in sight. The young man was someone who wouldn't stop until whatever he was doing was done. He wasn't done, so he kept at it until dusk arrived. Now, his stomach was hungry, and he was exhausted. He made a fire and baked a tuber. After eating, he figured he'd dig up some more so he could show the out-sized tubers to the villagers, who, no doubt, had never seen any so large. Excited, he asked himself, "How big could *this* tuber be?" Minutes later he was sound asleep.

He woke up, and cried out: "Ah! It is already dawn!" He got up quickly, and began working. But no matter how hard he put his back into it, he couldn't reach the other end of the especially big tuber. After two days of this, the portion of the tuber he could see so far would be more than he could handle in terms of lugging it back home. "What should I do?" he asked himself. His answer was to continue digging. He reasoned that once he had unearthed the entire tuber, he'd leave it there and carry home what was already in the basket. Later, he'd ask the villagers to come back and help him, and he'd divide up the giant tuber evenly among them.

That was his decision, this hard-working, overly stubborn young man. But he still had a problem. "Whoa!" he exclaimed, when suddenly he realized that one of his feet was sticking into the air. He quickly gripped the tuber, looking down; this made no sense. "Oh my, there is nothing beneath me!" He took a closer look, and saw another bright blue sky, one that was not his own. The only thing visible near him was the tuber. "Where does this tuber grow to?" he asked. It was indeed a very long, very strange *ta'eucu* tuber.

Yes, he was a man full of curiosity and stubbornness; he always wanted to explore and get to the very bottom of things. So of course he wanted to follow this tuber down into the new bright blue sky, to see what was underneath. However, on the other hand, he told himself, you have been away from home for two days. He was missing his parents, his beautiful wife, and his two lovely kids; they must have missed him too. After further serious thinking, he decided to head home. He grabbed onto the tuber and began to climb up along it. Up and up he went, until he was very tired and couldn't climb any farther, due of course to all the hard work he had put in over the last several days. Then he suddenly lost his grip on the tuber and proceeded to slide down, and down. After who knew how long, he hit something that resulted in acute pain on his bottom. And he passed out.

After some time, he wasn't sure how long, he woke up, probably the result of the extreme fragrance of something he smelled somewhere nearby. More amazing than the fragrance, at first, was what he saw: a group of children; no, it was a group of dwarfs who surrounded him! Each one stood motionless, starring at him wide-eyed, with some exhibiting signs of real anxiety. He stood up with considerable difficulty—his butt was still killing him—and let his nose lead him in the direction of the strong fragrance, which he could no longer resist. The dwarfs followed him at a safe distance. However, because they were so short—the tallest one only came up to about his waist—they required several steps to each of his in order to keep up. Over time, the group of dwarfs grew larger, and some now carried weapons, including three-foot-long spears. They watched the young man carefully.

Still following the direction of the fragrance, he stopped in front of a small thatch house. There, he saw a group of female dwarfs steaming rice. How delicious the smell was! he thought. His hungry stomach began to make a *"guru, guru"* noise. But because he was a mannered man, he wouldn't take anything from anyone else unless it was offered to him. Finally, he just sat down on the ground. The dwarfs were relieved by his non-aggressive behavior, and went about their business.

Before long, he saw something quite strange. The dwarfs, surrounding a pot without a cover, leaned toward the steam and opened their mouths, then closed their mouths, then opened them, over and over again. What on earth were they doing? When the steam from the open pot was gone, the dwarfs dispersed.

The dwarfs didn't invite him to open his mouth—for steam or anything else—so he endured the hunger he was experiencing. He took note of his surroundings. The sky looked the same as the sky at home; there were trees, and flowers on the ground; however, the rice fields and gardens were very small. He walked around, and was followed by the dwarfs wherever he went. He found some wild fruits and picked some to eat. He wouldn't touch any farm crops because he was a mannered man. He walked to a farm, and noticed that there were no paddy rice fields, only dry ones like the villagers at home used to grow as the first crop of the season. But wait a second! he thought to himself. The dwarfs' rice was not smooth, as he was accustomed to, but had a hairy structure on the grain. What kind of rice was this? He was also very surprised that the dwarfs grew few crops other than rice.

It was getting dark, and he missed his family very much. Of course, he was not alone. The dwarfs, both adults and children, now felt comfortable enough to approach him, and did so tentatively, waving their hands, laughing, and gibbering. Yes, the giant tuber was still there. But he was hungry, and exhausted. He wouldn't have the energy to climb back up the tuber to reach home without a few days rest.

At night, the dwarfs slept inside their tiny houses, while the young man slept outside. The next morning, he observed them surrounding the rice steamer again. They opened their mouths as wide as they would go, and breathed in deeply, just like they'd done the day before. After watching them for a while, he realized they didn't actually consume the rice, but simply inhaled the fragrant steam. After they were "full," they walked away from the steamer. He took this opportunity to grab a handful of rice and stuff it into his mouth. "Ahhh!" he cried out. It was actually sticky rice, and was much more fragrant and tenderly chewy than the sticky rice at home. Those dwarfs were amazed—shocked really—by the way he was eating it, and watched him wide-eyed while saying things to each other like "*chi, chi, za, za*" and other words that he did not understand in the slightest.

At the moment he couldn't have cared less what they thought about him. This was the most enjoyable rice meal he ever had had in his life! The rice was extremely delicious; yam-free rice meal![18] At home, he wouldn't dare to eat so much rice without having yam in it as a filler. Well, he proceeded to eat so much that he needed to find a toilet. But since the dwarfs' restrooms were too tiny for him to enter, he had no choice but to squat on the ground. The dwarfs were curious as to what

---

18. *In general, rice was more expensive than yam in Taiwan, therefore relatively poor families would add yam to the rice so that they didn't have to use as much rice, to stretch the meal.*

he was doing. Suddenly they yelled, "Whoa!" They had never seen such big feces! Theirs was about the size of rat poop.

Because of the delicious steamed sticky rice, he decided without hesitation to stay and help the dwarfs eat their rice. It would be a pity and a waste to throw away such yummy rice. He studied their behavior, made friends with them, and occasionally did some work for them. In their eyes, he was a goodhearted giant, a Hercules. He was very well liked, especially by the children, who enjoyed climbing on him.

A long time had passed, and again he began to sorely miss his home village, his parents, wife, and his two lovely kids. The dwarfs wanted him to stay, but he insisted on leaving. By that time they were harvesting the first rice crop of the year, so he grabbed a bunch of rice seeds to plant when he got home. But the dwarfs forbade him from doing so. There was no resolving the conflict. Every time he tried to grab some rice seeds, the dwarfs rushed him. Even though his body was much larger than theirs, he couldn't handle the discomfort caused by these small people, who crawled over him like ants. Finally, he gave up—or pretended to. As a result, the dwarfs stopped monitoring him. Later, while they weren't paying attention, he stole some rice seeds and put them in his pocket, inside his ears, and even up his rectum, anywhere he could think of to hide them. Then he took off. He climbed up the *ta'eucu*, and had gotten quite high by the time the dwarfs discovered what he was up to. They yelled "*wah la, wah la,*" whatever that meant, at him from below. Some of them even attempted to climb the *ta'eucu*, but it was too big for them to hold on to so they fell down to the ground without having gotten very far.

As he was departing—climbing up and away from the dwarfs and their upside-down sky—the young man cut off the *ta'eucu* beneath him so that the dwarfs couldn't use it. He followed the hole he'd dug before, and climbed back up to the ground surface where he had begun his adventure. He removed from all his hiding places the sticky rice seeds he had stolen, and wrapped them carefully with a taro leaf. He was delighted by this miraculous journey, and pleased to have returned safely. Mostly, though, he was pleased to have successfully stolen the seeds of the fragrant sticky rice.

He looked around the ground. His basket was still there; however, the *ta'eucu* he had dug up before was all rotten. He decided to dig some fresh *ta'eucu* and carry it home. His family members, seeing him return after having vanished for so many days, were delighted, as were the villagers. They all marveled at the story of his miraculous journey, and hearing about his eating so much fragrant sticky steamed rice made their mouths water. He consoled them, though, saying: "Rest assured! I have stolen some seeds. Once I have harvested enough from them, I will share with you all, and you will all enjoy the fragrant sticky steamed rice as much as I did!"

The Tsou's Legendary Tales and Customs

Beginning

Amo Hamo (天神哈莫 in Mandarin Chinese),[19] the supreme god, was standing on the top of Mt. Patunkuonu,[20] gently shaking a maple tree. Tree seeds were flaking down and became humans who propagated. Amo Hamo told these people to form *hosas*, or communities, so that the tribal people could live together. What follows is the fairy tale told by the Tsou people about the origin of their ancestors. Although the tale is mythical, there is no doubt that many Tsou people today firmly believe that Mt. Patunkuonu is their ancestral home.

Later—no one is sure how many years later—according to the myth, the earth was totally inundated. People and animals who were used to roaming the forests watched as the flood waters continued to rise, immersing first the smaller mountains, then the larger ones, and finally all of them—except Mt. Patunkuonu. So the animals and humans rushed there to escape the calamity. It was told that the people who escaped to Mt. Patunkuonu from the floods included the Tsou, and other tribes. In addition, there was a wide variety of beasts and worms. The human survivors, who cherished life, endeavored to live togeth-

---

19. *Generally speaking, "Mandarin Chinese" refers to the spoken Chinese dialect that is currently used as an official language, while "Chinese" can be written Chinese or the collection of all spoken Chinese dialects. The distinction is a loose and subtle one.*
20. *The present name is Mt. Jade (玉山).*

er peacefully. This is the second mythological story that is part of the Tsou's history relating to Mt. Patunkuonu.

In the Tsou's language, despite its rather limited vocabulary, there are specific proper nouns associated with Mt. Jade, as well as writings depicting historical events and citing nearby place names. For example, Mt. Jade, called Putunkuonu in the Tsou language (later it was translated to 八通關 in Mandarin), is adjacent to a mountain called Tataka (塔塔加). A Tsou song titled "Mountain Climbing" contains these lines: "In the days of clear skies, look to the east where the sun rises; one can see Hwalien (花蓮). Look to the west where the sun sets; one can see the big ocean." This indicates that the Tsou people once were active in the Mt. Jade area. The history of Mt. Jade and the Tsou people is clearly interrelated, and in the Tsou's view Mt. Jade is sacred.

Legend has it that as the floods receded, the lucky Tsou survivors descended Mt. Patunkuonu in groups on separate routes designated

Mt. Jade (painting by the translator)

by family name. Some followed the C'eha no mokvou River (陳有蘭溪) all the way downstream to the Jo-Shuei River (濁水溪) and surrounding areas that today are known as Gi-gi (集集) and Doh-nan (斗南). Some groups followed the Nanzusian River (南梓仙溪), even as far as the Lau-lung River (荖濃溪); some groups were tossed about along the Tzeng-Wen River (曾文溪) to arrive at Tainan (台南), or continue all the way to An-Ping (安平); and some

The author strolling on an ancient mountain trail in 2020.

groups followed the Ching-suei River (清水溪) to the Chia-yi Plain (嘉義平原). Groups with different family names gradually settled down along various rivers, creeks, and streams where it was arable—to burn and cultivate the land, or hunt. Over a long period of time, they formed settlements and established *hosas*. From as far north as the Jo-Shuei River (濁水溪) to as far south as the debouchure of the Tzeng-Wen River (曾文溪) and the An-Ping (安平) area, there are Tsou footprints and ancient stories.

According to legends, Amo Hamo was a giant. He led the Tsou people on their descent from Mt. Jade in a search for a new world where they could settle and propagate. He stamped down towering mountains into flat lands to make the area more livable. He decided where Tsou of high social status would live, as well as those whose family names were less worthy or distinguished.

When Amo Hamo descended from Mt. Jade, His Majesty's first footstep was in the area of what today is known as the Tfuya Community (特富野部落), which is located in the Tapangu (達邦) Community in the

Alishan (阿里山) region of Chia-yi County (嘉義縣). His second footstep was on the Tapangʉ Community. According to legend, when He was descending from Mt. Jade, He was looking in a westerly direction while His two feet were standing at these two spots, just a few kilometers apart. His third footstep landed on Seya'funu (石棹) of the Chung-her Village (中和村) in Chia-yi (嘉義), which is only about ten kilometers away from Tapangʉ. The fourth footstep was much farther: He stepped on Gung-tien Village (公田村) in Fang-lu Township (番路鄉), while the next footstep crushed the foothill of Hohcʉbʉ (塔山). Step by step, He stamped out areas that were suitable for the Tsou families. He instructed the people to establish communities, and called upon Millet Goddess *Nivnu* (尼弗奴) to teach the Tsou life skills and cultivating techniques so that they could live a good life—wherever it was they were told to live.

Over time, some of these small settlements gradually became *hosas* (大社, Head Communities), which were—and still are—centers of tradition, culture, education, and the military; they are also in control of various Branch Communities.[21] Every *hosa* has a *peongsi*, or chief, who serves as the leader, also called *Tou-moo* (頭目), of the community. The *peongsi's* responsibilities include leading battles, guarding hunting grounds, settling disputes with other tribes or *hosas,* hosting tribal ceremonies, handling affairs of crime and punishment, and making decisions regarding important ceremonies and major events. For all the *peongsi's* apparent power, he can't become a dictator because all major decisions have to first be approved by the elders in their council meetings.

---

21. *While the literal translations of the terms* 大社 *and* 小社 *are Large Community and Small(er) Community, the difference between the two is not just their size. A Large Community also serves a lead decision making role and has authority over several smaller communities. Therefore, for the sake of clarity, the terms Head Community and Branch Community instead of Large Community and Small Community were used.*

The head of a *hosa* is required to have good leadership qualities, and the ability to make the scattered smaller communities (小社) cohesive parts of the entire community, willing to work together wholeheartedly with and be receptive and loyal to the *hosa*. The head man must notify the scattered families of both high and low social status whenever the *hosa* is making major decisions, and ask for the family's participation in any decision making process.

However, due to a population continually on the move, some Tsou people disappeared, while others remained. A case in point: When the Japanese ruled, several thousand Tsou were moved to reside in San-ming Village (三民鄉) and Tao-yuan Village (桃源鄉) in Kao-hsiung (高雄); both districts belong to the Bunun tribe (布農族). In addition, many Bunun people were relocated to the area of C'eha no mokvou River (陳有蘭溪) in Nan-tou (南投), which was originally Tsou territory. The Tsou and Bunun people gradually adopted to their new environments, and became assimilated into existing populations in both language and lifestyle.

Apart from shifting demographics, battles with other tribes and epidemics caused the Tsou's population to decline and the areas in which they lived to shrink. As of today[22], there are only two *hosas* existent—Tfuya and Tapangu—along with six smaller communities. The total population, including Tsou scattered about in Nan-tou (南投) and Kao-hsiung (高雄), is some five to six thousand. Every year at the annual Harvest Festival (豐年祭) and Warrior Festival (戰祭), those who live in Nan-tou and Kao-hsiung and who still identify themselves as Tsou, return to find their roots and participate in the festivals.

---

22. *Circa 2003.*

Ceremonies and Rituals

The Tsou's ceremonial rituals and festivals were closely intertwined with the people's daily lives.[23] For example, in order to have hope for a good harvest, millet and rice ceremonies were conducted; to help ensure a successful hunt, there was a hunting ceremony; to aspire to win a battle over foreigners or to commemorate a past victory, there was, and still is, the Warrior Festival; to realize peace in one's residence, there was a peace-seeking ceremony; to garner safety while using a road, there was a road blessing ceremony; and to worship the great Mother Nature there is still a ritual to honor the earth.

In order to facilitate a long-overdue repair of a *kuba*, there is a repair ceremony. As implied by its name, a *kuba* is an education center where men, and only men, could go to engage in activities related to learning about and carrying on the Tsou culture and heritage. Of course this shows the Tsou to be a paternal society. In recent times, due to more outsiders visiting the Tsou communities who are not familiar with Tsou customs, a sign "Women Are Not Allowed" is posted on a wooden pole in front of the building.

While each and every ceremony is extremely important, in the past the one that was paid the most attention—related as it was to

---

23. *While various ceremonial rituals are still practiced today, they differ in many ways from the old, traditional ones.*

the tribe's livelihood—was the ritual for the millet barn. Historically the primary food staples of the Tsou were millet, yam, and dried land-rice, all blessings of the Goddess Nivnu (尼弗奴). The paddy-rice field was introduced by the Han people after the Tsou's contacts with them. Because of this, rituals for the millet barn were practiced much earlier and were more closely observed than the rituals for the rice barn. One is greatly touched knowing how the rituals, from those for seed selection to seed spreading, are treated with such thoughtfulness and care, as evidenced by the profound respect for and humility shown to the Goddess Nivnu. After about six months of a year's hard work, and as an expression of their gratefulness for the millet harvest, all of the Tsou dance and celebrate at the *Homeyaya* (Harvest Festival) until dawn.

Another relatively major ceremony is the *Mayasbi* (Warrior Festival). Its program is similarly rich and solemn; its main purpose is to worship Amo Hamo and the warriors.

Due to a well-developed transportation network, today the Tsou commonly receive a contemporary education. In addition, highly developed information technologies have enabled them to shift from their former and traditional self-sufficient lifestyles to very different ways of living and farming. These days, they seldom grow millet as a food staple; rather, it is used primarily for ceremonial and brewing purposes. And they now grow crops of higher economic value—such as tea, vegetables suitable for growth in high-latitude climates, and flowers—to sell in order to then purchase other life necessities.

Because the Tsou society has evolved into a diversified one, a lot of young people work in a variety of professions outside their tribal land areas. Their schedule regarding work and leisure is governed no longer by the tribal dictates of planting and harvesting ceremonies once held seasonally throughout the year. As a result, the practice of *homeyaya* isn't emphasized as it was in the past, while today the ceremony of *Mayasbi* possess greater importance.

Before a *Mayasbi* is performed, the *hosa* leader or *Tou-moo* (頭目) of the Large Community calls a planning meeting to be held at the *kuba* by notifying the kinship units of different family names to send their

Kuba, education center for the young men and young men only.

representatives. The first item on the agenda is to review and discuss anything that has happened—major or minor, good or bad—to the entire tribe during the year. After assessing the situation, they determine how the *Mayasbi* should proceed, how the planned events should be sequenced, and how tasks should

Mayasbi, Warrior Festival. Held on February 15th annually.

be divided among the participants. Occasionally, when issues don't have definitive answers, assistance is sought from a seer.

A sketch of *Mayasbi* by Ms. Hsin-I Tseng, a writer and a lecturer on novel writing.

Also, before a *Mayasbi* is held some elders would find time on an evening out of their busy work schedules to meet at a *kuba* to help young men rehearse the songs to be sung at the *Mayasbi*. According to the old customs, the

Mayasbi, Warrior Festival. Male members.

songs that were sung at ceremonies were forbidden to be sung at other occasions; doing so would show great disrespect to the gods. However, these days, in order for people living outside Tsou communities to be exposed to Tsou culture, groups of aboriginals often perform their old ceremonies outside Tsou communities, and even overseas.

In the old days, before ceremonies could be performed men from different family names in a *hosa* were required to hunt, in order to store meat for the occasion. This required that roads from a *hosa* to the hunting ground be cleared, and prayers said to ensure a successful hunt. Also, tribal members of the Branch Communities were responsible for cleaning up the roads leading from Branch Communities to the Head Community, which also was carried out during the Ceremony for Roads. The women were busy too, husking millet to make millet wine for entertaining the guests, and for the tribal members of Head and Branch communities after they attended the ceremonies.

All Tsou ceremonies are performed in the utmost sacred manner. Those present should be quiet; even sneezing is not allowed. There are also strict requirements regarding attendance. Non-Tsou tribe members, people who have violated tribal rules, and relatives of natural disaster victims are not welcome. Toward the end of each sub-section of a ceremony, there are often short but loud outbursts of howling by the participants intended to express their god-fearing respect, and at the same time alert participants of the imminent closing of the sub-section. Before the closure of the entire ceremony, the chief leads the participants in singing somewhat lighthearted songs, dealing with subjects such as history, youth, warriors, and others.

Before the formal *Mayasbi*, or Warrior Ceremony, is conducted, a ceremony is held for the Men's Meeting Place, so that it's functional, clean, and looks presentable. First, the ceremonial master consecrates the site by sprinkling wine upon it. Then he orders young people to climb to the rooftop to remove the sacred flower, the Dendrobium comatum (木槲蘭).[24] Next, the young people remove the old thatch from the roof and install a new layer. Finally, the sacred flower is replaced where it had been previously, or a new one is planted at the same spot.

---

24. *A species of orchids native to Taiwan, Dendrobium comatum is the Tsou's tribal flower.*

Both sides of the building entrance are also adorned with the same plants. If major repairs to the *kuba* are deemed necessary, they should be completed way ahead of the scheduled ceremony.

All participants are required to dress in traditional Tsou costume, which consists of a sword and a sacred flower to adorn their leather caps. The flowers are freshly picked by the participants early on the morning of the ceremony, from deep in the mountains. They also dye red the dried bark of stripped hibiscus stems and tie them to their arms and hunting-knife straps. The participants follow the chief in a procession into the *kuba* to pick pieces of burning charcoal from the fire pit, in which an ever-burning fire is maintained to symbolize that the Tsou tribe will live on forever. They carry the burning charcoal to use as tinder for another fire pit that is located at the central area of the ceremonial ground; this pit is laid beforehand with wood to burn as the sacred fire. Then, the ceremonial participants face the sacred tree, a large-leafed banyan.

Following this is a ceremony to welcome the gods' spirits. In the past, a wild boar was slaughtered and each warrior would dip his sword into the animal's blood and spread it upon the sacred tree to honor the gods. Today, a pig is used in the ceremony; it is usually home-raised and not wild. The chief then orders several strong warriors to climb the sacred tree and, on the way up, clear the branches to symbolize clearing a path for the gods to descend from the heaven to the earth. In the branch-clearing process, three branches are left untouched: one points to the *kuba*, one to the chief's residence, and the third to the tribe's residential area. Small pieces of pork speared by wood sticks are placed on the trunk of the sacred tree as a gesture of invitation to the gods' spirits. The ceremony participants then form a semicircle, hand-in-hand, facing the sacred tree while the chief leads them in god-inviting songs to welcome the arrival of Amo Hamo and the warriors.

Next on the ceremonial agenda is the Tribal Solidarity Ceremony. Once again, the participants enter the *kuba*. The elders who represent various family names decorate the rooftop with sacred flowers, and return to the sacred tree to share more flowers with the participating young warriors. With flowers in hand, each warrior runs to their family's millet barn to declare that Amo Hamo has blessed the family. Obtaining a small bamboo cup of millet wine from their respective homes, the young warriors run back to the *kuba* and empty the cup into a large bamboo jar stored inside a sacred cabinet. This is done to symbolize solidarity among the kinship units, or descendants of a particular family name. The wine in the large bamboo jar, collected from all the household units, is then shared by the ceremonial participants from all of the different kinship family units.

There are two other ceremonial rituals that are performed during the Tribal Solidarity Ceremony to bless a family's line of succession from generation to generation. One of them is the ritual for a newborn male infant to enter the *kuba* for the first time. The infant is carried into the *kuba* either by his father, or by his uncle, along with a cup of wine. The household elder touches the infant's head to signify that he has been accepted into the community and to bless him with a healthy and harmonious life while growing up.

The second ritual is the initiation rite for boys 15 or 16 years of age. The elder sings war and hunting songs, and the participants sing along with him. The elder whips the boy's bottom while at the same time admonishing him. Boys who had behaved themselves receive symbolic lashes, while boys who didn't behave receive heavy lashes, to teach them a lesson. The purpose of this rite is to warn the teenagers that since they are now grown up they must obey the tribe's rules, work hard, and learn to behave responsibly—towards their family, the tribal community, and themselves. The young men hope this will be the last time they'll be physically punished. While this ritual is in progress, the ceremonial master has each member stamp on the *kuba's* floor while striking it with a wooden stick. The elder then leads the group to the millet barn of the household that was established the earliest and has contributed the most to the community. After this, they visit the house of the community chief, and sip from the wine container held by the chief. Finally, they go home and put on adult dress and return to the *kuba*.

At the time when the initiation rite for male youths is being held, a parallel one for young women is held at the chief's house, and is conducted by the wife of the chief to teach young ladies their duties as women. After a long "admonition" session, the chief's wife puts scarves on the young ladies' heads (before they officially become women, they don't need to wear scarves), and leads them to the ceremonial ground at the *kuba* to join post-ceremony dancing and singing.

After the arrival of the gods via the ceremonies of invitation, there are the ceremonies for sending away the gods. Here, the participants return to the ceremonial ground facing the *kuba* in a half circle, and sing Songs of Farewell to send off Amo Hamo and the warrior gods back to heaven. Two young ladies each carries a torch to the ceremonial ground and lays it in the fire pit to signify that we women have our role in carrying on the Tsou's legacy. The ladies then join the procession of sending the gods on their way.

In addition to the Ceremony for Roads, conducted before the greater ceremony begins, as mentioned earlier, the participating kinship units carry a bunch of thatch and go to their own community square in the suburb near where they live; wine toasts are made to the community gods in hopes they grant the people daily safe passage on the roads. They then return to the *kuba* ceremonial ground.

The last ceremony is the Ceremony for Kinship's Millet Barn. Here, the chief leads the participants to the various millet barns in all the kinship family units, and conducts wine toasts to thank the gods, with much gratitude, while beseeching them to continue to bless the people with bountiful harvests in the coming years.

Customs – Praise the Life

1. Birth

The Tsou are a patriarchal society. To hunt, farm, and fend off foreign invaders requires a sufficiently large tribal population. Therefore, the society encourages women to reproduce prolifically, and for that reason pregnancies are of great importance. Custom has it that in order to give birth to strong and healthy infants, women must observe some taboos. When pregnant, for example, they should not catch and slaughter animals, or touch weapons and hunting gear that are used by men, and they should not attend ceremonies.

In Tsou tribes, there are no professionally trained midwives; elder women usually deliver the babies. Mothers normally teach their daughters how to deliver babies themselves—a precaution stemming from the fear that no one be around to help when a woman gives birth. One week after a baby is born, the umbilical cord is severed and thrown to the top of the roof. Legend has it that the cord will become a gecko. Therefore, when geckos are spotted and heard making sounds on the walls of a house or ceiling, children, for fun, try to guess which gecko came from whose umbilical cord, based upon the lizard's size. (While geckos in Southern Taiwan can make a vocal sound, those in Northern Taiwan cannot.)

On the infant's first birthday, the grandfather on the mother's side gives the grandson a model arrow-and-bow set, encouraging him to become a warrior and super hunter; to the granddaughter he would give a small spade, in hopes that she become a hardworking woman.

When the child is 15 or 16 years of age, they will visit the maternal grandpa again, and receive blessings on becoming an adult.

2. Wedding Ceremony

Tsou marital customs dictate that tribal members be monogamous. Traditionally, a marital relationship is not only a matter between a man and a woman, but also a major event between two families and the place where each grew up.

When a young man becomes interested in a young lady, or when a couple of young people have been deeply in love, a matchmaker—they are mostly men—will bring wine to the young lady's family and offer a marriage proposal on the young man's behalf. The lady's family will then invite familial elders to attend the occasion, for several reasons: to show respect to the elders, and to strengthen their bargaining power. Sometimes, even though the lady's family is in fact in favor of the marriage proposal, they may pretend that they are surprised by it; they may even criticize or say negative things about the man, and nit-pick about things in general. But the marriage proposal team[25] members might play dumb, pretending they don't understand what the lady's side is being so fussy about, while at the same time saying nice things and urging everyone to drink. This process keeps going for a long time. If the lady's side shows enthusiasm too early in the process, that could make people suspicious and wonder whether there is something wrong with the young lady. When the lady's family pretend that they are not wholeheartedly willing to accept the marriage proposal, but will nonetheless, the man's team will present the lady's family with a piece of black fabric as a gift, and invite them to return with them to the young man's home. A date will then be chosen for the wedding festival, allowing time to invite friends and families.

After the man's team brings the young lady to his home, the man and the lady sit on either side of the matchmaker. The matchmaker gives each some sticky rice cake, blesses them with goodwill, and admonishes them. Finally, he escorts them into the new bedroom. On occasion, it happens that a groom or a bride is too shy to enter the room with an opposite sex—especially under the eager eyes of the many who are watching—and runs away from the scene. When this happens, there are people to usher the couple back into the bedroom. Only then is the matchmaker's job considered accomplished.

The next day, the new mother-in-law leads the daughter-in-law to the paddy rice field to work, albeit symbolically. On the third day, the bride's family members visit the groom's family bringing millet wine

---

25. *Author's note: It is not just the matchmaker who presents the marriage proposal, but the man's side will also invite relatives who are distinguished and influential members of the community, to go along with him.*

and sticky rice cake as gifts, and invite the bride and the groom to return with them to their house. Similarly, the father-in-law will take the new son-in-law to the mountains to collect fire wood to show that he has accepted the son-in-law.

In the Tsou's tradition, when a marriage proposal is presented, both sides agree upon certain marriage commitments. Unlike the tradition of the Han people, a dowry and betrothal money are not required. However, to show the proper gratitude for the bride's family having raised her, the groom will commit to providing assistance to the bride's family, called *fifiho* in the Tsou language. The commitment may last for one year, two years, or even as long as three to five years. During that time, the husband lives in the house of the wife's family. When there are major events in the husband's family, both husband and wife and their children must attend the events. When the committed time period is up, the parents of the husband, bearing gifts such as wine and rice cake, go to the daughter-in-law's family to welcome home their son, daughter-in-law, and their grandchildren.

3. Funeral Ceremony

Over time, the encroachment of the modern world upon Taiwan would put an end to many of its old customs, including those governing burials. Before the Tsou had accepted the modern ways of living, however, after a family member died the deceased was dressed in traditional clothing while the body was still flexible. With the help of a wood frame, the corpse was fixed in an upright squatting position with both arms crossing the chest. A hole was dug in the house and the body was buried in the hole in the same upright position. A fire pit was maintained above the hole, or burial site, to keep the ground dry; it would take some time initially for the damp earth to dry out. Family members slept by the fire pit to comfort the deceased. When buried, the body would face Hohcʉbʉ—the sacred mountain for the dead, which is located southwest of today's Alishan tourist area—so that it would be easier for the spirit of the dead to go home in order to rest.

Normally, family members continued to live in the house until so many holes had been dug there was no more room for the dead. The living would then search for a new site to build their new house. They'd leave the old house behind for trees and grass to take over.

The Tsou's tradition had it that once a person passed away, the body should be buried as soon as possible, lest it emit foul odors; this would be regarded as disrespectful to the deceased, and would likely elicit criticism by the tribal members. Therefore, before the area's transportation network became functional and convenient, people would rely on their feet to get from one location to another, and it was permissible to bury the dead before all of the relatives had arrived to attend the burial ceremony. Even so, the relatives, upon hearing the news, had to hurry if they wanted to arrive in time to console one another.

In the past, within five days of the burial the family members of the deceased were prohibited from consuming fish, meat, or alcohol, and were not permitted to speak loudly, work, or howl out loud to express their grief. The entire atmosphere was to remain very solemn. On the fifth day, the relatives would gather together again, along with a seer to conduct the ceremony, and sprinkle wine above the burial site,[26] and honor the dead with cooked sticky rice.

---

26. Today the Tsou bury their dead in a cemetery, following the example of the Han.

Much was done before a burial ceremony to make things ready. For example, family members placed a section of crushed bamboo and thatch by the front door, and a bamboo cup of wine by the entrance in the back of the house. The seer fashioned a hideout using a haystack, from which he suddenly jumped, then picked up and struck the bamboo and thatch, and yelled: "Go away and do not return to bother the family members!" He emptied the wine on the ground, and circled the house with strings of thatch to indicate that the deceased would no longer be welcome to the house. In addition, he used bunches of thatch to sweep around the house and lightly brush the family members to chase the spirits away from them. When the seer had finished, the attending relatives circled the fire pit and drank a little wine.

On the sixth day, the female family members would clean up the house, inside and out, and wash the clothes. Male members fished in the brooks, and broiled and consumed whatever they caught onsite. They'd head home the next morning with thatch tied onto their clothes, and then go out again hunting, and sleep in the mountains. On the eighth day, life for everyone in the tribe would return to normal.

****

In summary: Today, as a result of frequent contact with people outside the Tsou tribe, along with the advancement of information technologies, many rather good customs have gradually been forgotten, the Warrior Festival being an exception. We, the Tsou people, should reflect on this serious state of affairs.

2. My Homeland

A River Section That Belonged To My Family

In the long past, when the population of the Tsou was relatively small and the land was expansive—before it was intruded upon and occupied by outsiders—the land was divided up based upon a family's size and used for their support as a hunting ground (*hupa* in the Tsou's language) and for farming.

Rivers (*c'oeha*) were also divided into sections for family use. In principle, families whose land was close to a river were entitled to own a section of the river adjacent to that land; families who were first to move by a river had the right to own a certain section of a river as well. As for smaller brooks (*va'ahʉ*), that would depend on who were the owners of the lands on both sides of the brooks. If the lands on both sides belonged to the same owner, that section of the river would belong to the owner. If they belonged to different owners, then that section of the river was co-owned by them.

As noted, in times past the land was distributed among the Tsou people based upon family size. Back then, there was no precision survey equipment; mountain spines and valleys were used as property lines. As for the rivers, initially stacked stones were used to delineate property lines. As landowners became more familiar with a particular area, they would remember who owned what section of a river, even if the stacked stones had been washed away by floods.

Please don't think the Tsou people were selfish or overbearing, claiming river sections for themselves to use as they pleased. Their system of land and water use was based upon tradition, spanning thousands of years during which time many generations relied solely on the earth for their sustenance. Respect for nature, they realized, showed great wisdom; therefore the Tsou "borrowed" natural resources, paying nature back by taking care of it and obeying its cycles and rhythms.

Since there was no system of writing to chronicle the knowledge and experience of past generations, an oral history of the Tsou was passed down instead. The Tsou acknowledged the interdependence of nature and themselves, stressing the need for harmony and unwavering respect for the natural world in which they—and their descendants—lived. The purpose behind the distribution of mountain lands and rivers to families was to enable humans to endlessly propagate, and in so doing bear the responsibility of protecting animals from extinction while ensuring the balance of ecological resources.

In the primitive Tsou culture, there was no monetary system. While people sometimes bartered for what they needed, they were mainly self-sufficient. Millet and yams, for example, would be farmed on a small piece of land in quantities just enough to feed a family for a year. They didn't wish to destroy mountains and forests to cultivate more land than necessary, let alone for the purpose of trading for a profit. Hunting, farming, fishing, and day-to-day living were conducted in accordance with the seasons of the year. This, they believed, was a gift from The Creator to humans and nature. The changing seasons of the year dictated what human actions were appropriate. In the spring, there was no hunting in order that animals might freely breed. After autumn harvest, the land needed a rest, and was allowed to lay fallow.

Of course it wasn't a good idea to catch fish and shrimps at times when they carried eggs and roe!

The Tzeng-Wen River (*atuhcu c'oeha* 曾文溪)[27] originates from the Tsang-Gu-Tsuan River (*toeku* 長谷川溪) between Sueh-Shan (*t'ut'ubuhu* 水山) and Sia-Shan (*maeno* 霞山) in the Alishan (*psaseongana* 阿里山) mountain range. When the Tzeng-Wen River reaches the Da-Bang Community (*hosa tapangʉ* 達邦社) in Alishan Village, it merges with the *Yiskiana* River (伊西基阿那溪), becoming the Da-Bang section of the Tzeng-Wen River. Heading southwest, it becomes the Ler-Yeh (*lalauya* 樂野) section, and then the Shan-Mei (*saviki* 山美) section, Shin-Mei (*oi'iana* 新美) section, and finally the Tsar-Shan (*cayamavana* 茶山) section. Some seven to eight kilometers past the Tsar-Shan section, it reaches the Tzeng-Wen Great Dam (曾文水庫).

In the area named Chu-Giao (*pcopcoknu* 竹腳) of the Ler-Yeh (*lalauya* 樂野) section, there was a river section assigned to my ancestors. When I was a child, this section was more than 100 kilometer wide. Today, continual flooding, caused by over-logging and resultant erosion, has made it much wider.

From the source of the Tzeng-Wen River to the Tzeng-Wen Great Dam, there are numerous smaller brooks which merged into our river section. The Vokudana Brook, which originates from Lake Ler-Yeh (樂野湖), joins together with the Tzeng-Wen River. Here, fish and shrimps were abundant.

---

27. *In general, with some exceptions, the first name noted in parentheses is the aboriginal, or Tsou, pronunciation of the mountain or river, followed by the current name in Chinese characters.*

In early days, before the time of over-logging, even small brooks, not just the Tzeng-Wen River, were rich in Xenocypris fish and river eels, who like the rock-climbing loaches loved clear, clean, and cool water. This is the greatest gift from The Great Creator!

Here are the fishing methods used by the Tsou people:

Harpoon fishing *(tufngi)*

This involves the harpooning of fish and shrimp while holding a torch. Whenever Father wanted to supplement the protein intake of family members, he figured the easiest way was to go harpoon fishing; for this he would use any spare time he had in the evening. (Harpoon fishing was a more convenient and agreeable means compared to slaughtering domestic birds; besides, a good supply of poultry was necessary for important festivals, and for unexpected family guests.) Father would pick up a couple of dried bamboo sticks from a pile of firewood to make a torch; he would then shoulder a container made of bamboo and carry the harpoon he had made to the river below our house. In around one hour—about the length of time it would take for the torch to burn out—he would return home with what would become a dish of delicacy for the following morning. Just the thought of it would send us into a beautiful night of sleep!

My father made all of his tools himself. Harpoons were relatively simple: He'd create four iron needles from wrought iron (the needles were a little thicker than tooth picks, about three to four inches long, and sharp on one end). He would tie the needles, evenly positioned and with the sharp ends pointing out, with hemp thread wound around one end of a slender bamboo stick or a solid miscanthus stem.

Of course, different sizes of harpoons were made for different sizes of intended prey. To spear shrimp or crab, too large a harpoon would make either delicacy pulpy and lose its flavor when cooked.

My father usually went harpooning after dinner. In those days, a flashlight was a thing of luxury; firewood, on the other hand, was abundant. Therefore, we used torches when we went fishing. If Father had the energy to fish longer in order to bring home more catches, he would ask my brother and me to carry spare torches, and follow him.

Once in a while, he would ask me to go with him no matter how tired I was—say, after a playful day (during my school years), or after a late, hard-working day (when I was working). I'd carry a 10-foot-long dried bamboo stick and follow him. I'd leap up and down on various sizes of rocks along the uneven stream banks—being extra careful to make sure that the ends of the bamboo stick didn't strike rocks or anything, lest the noise scare away any shrimp, crabs, or fish. They could dart away and hide very quickly.

Sometimes, if Father was doing well at a particular location, he would stay there longer. In places where there were large chunks of rock—dangerous for kids carrying a long bamboo stick—he would tell me to move to a safer spot. At times, I'd lie on a rock watching the night sky and the stars, wondering why they flickered and whether people some distance away could see our torches flickering as well. During those days, days of innocence and unruliness, all I knew about stars was that they were stars: I had no idea what they actually were. When I was really tired, I took a nap on a rock in the darkness of the wilderness, until my father called out to say it was time to go home.

Normally, Father kept his catches in a bamboo tube, which was made from sweet bamboo (麻竹). Sweet bamboo has large diameters and long sections between knots, and therefore are good for making bamboo tubes. To reduce a sweet bamboo's weight, the green outer layer was skinned. Shreds from rattan or wild hibiscus trunk bark were used to make a strap so that the bamboo tube could be carried, with the strap on one shoulder across the chest.

Later, an additional technique was added. A sheet of glass with a wooden frame would be held by hand and placed on the surface of water; despite the water running, things beneath the glass could still be clearly seen. Alas, this method could be used only during daytime. At night, with one hand holding a sheet of glass, another hand a harpoon, there was no hand left to hold a torch!

Fishing with fishing rods (*toa'lungu* 垂釣法)

My father wasn't very good at fishing with a rod, and that's why he admired the villager Otter Du. Mr. Du was called "Otter" for a good reason. Like otters, he understood the currents and was knowledge-able about the prey that lived in the water. Even when fishing was not in season, his fishing skills ensured that he would not go home empty handed.

Fish trap with beam structure (*siiungu* 魚槺法)

This fishing method was more time-consuming, but its use enabled a fisherman to take advantage of a longer season—from the fall when the water flow is moderate all the way to the dry season.

The first step in making a fishing rod in the old way was to collect the mountain palm fronds, strip the leaves, and lay out the stalks in the shape of a fan. The stalks were then woven and tied together with cords. A small round opening was made at the narrower end of the fan. The next step was to cut a section of sweet bamboo with several knots between the two ends. The knots, except the last one, would be broken clear; the last one was left together enough for water to run through, but with holes small enough so that the fish could not escape. The top end would be shredded and opened outward like the opening of a trumpet. These various parts were then brought to the site of the family-owned river section for final construction.

Having chosen a river section that was relatively flat with a water flow relatively moderate, a stone wall was built diagonally from one bank to the other across the stream, so that part of the water was directed towards a small channel flowing into the fish trap entrance. The entrance of the fish trap fence was fixed firmly with rocks, to support its placement in the stream. The small exit-end of the fan-shaped fence was aligned with the trumpet-shaped opening of the bamboo beam. The fence and the bamboo beam were firmed up and supported by other wooden beams, lest the whole thing be washed away by floods. Work on the structure was now completed, and ready for fish and shrimp to follow the stream right into the trap.

Only a small amount of water accompanying the fish and shrimp would flow into the bamboo, because most of the water would have flowed out between the palm stalks of the fence. Once the catch were inside the bamboo, they had nowhere to escape. This fishing method, while labor intensive, was a once-a-season construction project that allowed for fishing over a lengthy period of time. Another benefit was that the method didn't pose any danger of over-fishing, since some of the fish and shrimp would swim through the gaps between rocks, thus avoiding the trap entirely. Once the fishing season was over, the entire trap system was removed, and the stream restored to its original state— fish and shrimp could once again swim freely.

The best time to check for catches was in the early morning, because fish and shrimp were more likely to be caught at night, when they were more active. Besides, they would not have been as fresh if harvested in the afternoon.

Father liked to have us, boys and girls, with him when he worked; it seemed he didn't like to be alone. Being with him quite often, we learned a lot from the hardworking man! Because our house was about half an hour on foot from the fishing site, and because we didn't want to interfere with our regular day-time work, we normally went to check the traps around four o'clock in the morning. Since weather played a role in the activities of fish and shrimp, sometimes we didn't catch anything.

To gather what had been captured, we'd remove the bamboo from the stream, and peek into it to see what was inside. Sometimes, we caught river eels, which were slippery and moved vigorously, making them very difficult to handle. The best approach was to empty the contents in the bamboo onto a beach. An eel's sticky skin would be covered by sand, and it couldn't struggle for too long before it would succumb and die. Unfortunately, sticky skin with sand made it very difficult for us to clean it up later.

Diverting water away (涸溪法)

Possibilities abounded when flooding occurred! Sometimes, floods created double waterways on the riverbed. When that happened, one of them was blocked so that people could catch fish and shrimp. The riverbed was always restored afterwards.

Fishing with nets (*maaseu* 網撈法)

When a typhoon raged or when there was a big storm at the upper sections of a river, floods brought with them lots of soil making the water oxygen deficient and forcing organisms to surface—a good time to catch them.

During a typhoon, most people stayed in the house; however, my hardworking father would go to the rice field to check on the irrigation. He weathered the storm wearing a raincoat that was made of palm fibers, and brought with him his big homemade fishing net made of hemp strings, to net fish in the Tzeng-Wen River. When he was fishing, he only wore underwear. This made it easier for him to wade, and as he explained to us, it wouldn't matter much if he fell in! When his storage container was full, he'd remove his T-shirt and tie a knot at one end for extra storage room. Whenever I saw him coming home loaded with catch, the thought would come to my mind: How many risks had he taken to feed and care for the family?

When the catch was abundant, we normally seasoned the larger fish with salt or baked them, and cooked, stirred fried, or sun dried the shrimp. The food would be served as a delicacy, and enjoyed by all at festivals, special family occasions, or visits by friends from afar.

Sweeping method (掃地法)

This approach was used specifically to capture rock-climbing loaches. It worked like this: One person used a broom at the upper section of a stream to chase down the prey, while another captured them at the lower section of the stream. This was best done at night, when there was moonlight. Rock-climbing loaches were very tasty. Their abdomen is flat, and they have powerful sucking mouths—so powerful that they couldn't be easily removed from a rock when they were feeding on moss. Normally, we didn't see them swimming in the water unless they were caught in mud-carrying floods; this caused the oxygen deficiency I mentioned, forcing them to swim on the surface.

Bamboo fish trap (筌魚法)

To make this particular trap, bamboo was split along its grain into thin strips and woven together to make a trap with a large opening and a small end with no exit. Inside the entrance, a second layer of structure with shorter strips was woven that also had a large opening but with a small end with an exit. The structure was designed so that prey could get into the trap but couldn't return to escape through the entrance. Just secure it in the riverbed and check the catch each day! This method wasn't as elaborate as the fish trap with beam structure system.

Poisoning fish method (*otfo* 毒魚法)

The Tsou would put smashed roots of poisonous rattan[28] in the water to make prey groggy and slow, and easier to catch. This method wouldn't be carried out unless the downstream river-section owners

---

28. Derris trifoliate *in Latin.*

were notified first. It has been banned for a number of years for environmental and safety reasons.

The methods of fish trapping with beam structure, bamboo, water diversion, and sweeping could only be performed in one's own river section; otherwise, according to the Tsou's way of thinking, it was considered a violation of other people's rights.

Times have changed. Since mountains and rivers today are regarded as government property, the Tsou people have lost their *hupa* (hunting grounds); no family can claim that "It's my family's river." But I recall the days when Father fished in a stream section that was our own.[29]

---

29. *Most of the fishing methods can no longer be used today due to ecological degradation of the rivers. Today, people fishing with rods can be occasionally spotted.*

Memories of Bees

Every time I see a yellow flower, especially that tender, yellow, little chrysanthemum, it reminds me of my hometown. In the mountains each year in May and June, clusters of wild chrysanthemum flowers blossom under the sun, generously releasing their fragrance. However, maybe they are too abundant! They are not "sought-after" flowers, and few people stop and appreciate them, except the hardworking honey bees, working together in hundreds, happily gathering their pollen. The buzzing sounds from the bees' flapping wings can be heard at a distance. Their untiring endeavors will prepare them another year of good harvest, another winter worry-free.

While watching the bees tirelessly toiling, I am thinking of the beautiful color of the honey they make from the pollen of these wild yellow flowers.

Honey

Villagers in our community seldom raise honey bees. To harvest honey, one needs to wait for the spring season, after many kinds of flowers have already blossomed. Plum flowers are the first ones to bloom; the colder the weather, the more beautiful they become. The little bees are not afraid of the cold; as long as it's a nice day, they work energetically. Plum flowers are followed by, in order, prune, peach, and lychee flowers. In addition, there are flowers in the mountains from grass and trees according to the seasons, enough that there is abundant pollen for honey bees to collect. Thus, even after honey is harvested by humans, the tireless bees can continue to gather pollen and make more honey.

People are as diligent as bees when they harvest honey. By the time the sun dries up the dew, worker bees begin to look for flowers. Early in the morning, when the sun is only shining on parts of the mountains leaving other areas in shadow, one can easily see in the shadows the holes where bees are emerging. It doesn't take long to find the hives. This is the traditional method the Tsou people use to search for hives. They know the bees prefer to build their hives inside rock rifts or hollow tree trunks.

It's not that the villagers aren't motivated to search for beehives—who doesn't love sweet honey? Rather, their efforts are tempered by the profound understanding that bees and nature depend upon each other and maintain a homeostasis in ecology; it behooves humans to not disturb that vital interdependency. The Tsou know that honey bees are good for crops, flowers, and trees. When they accidentally discover a beehive while working in the mountains, then of course they will enjoy it!

All honey tastes sweet, but its flavor varies depending on the seasons of the year. The types of pollen bees gather determine the color and flavor of the honey they produce. What I miss the most today is the honey made from pollen produced by wild chrysanthemum flowers and their remarkable color: shiny with a faint tinge of yellow!

I still remember that indescribably satisfying sensation: holding a beehive loaded with honey and that honey, shining with that faint tinge of yellow, flowing to the palm of my hand and then between my fingers! That memory is still vivid in my mind. Royal jelly made from the pollen produced by the wild chrysanthemum is also tinged with yellow, its flavor richer than other kinds of honey.

Not sure why, but every time I see yellow chrysanthemums my mind is remembering those feelings and sensations: the flowers' charming color, the rich flavor of the honey they make. Sadly, these days because of over-logging and overdeveloping, it is not easy to find wild mums.

Big Wasps

Have you ever seen wasps (*veiio* in the Tsou language), also called bear bees or big yellow bees? Only once in a while do you see wasps as big and fatty as crickets. Their hives are also rarely seen; when I was a young girl, I only saw their hives twice. Because they have relatively large bodies, their hives are relatively large. Unlike Asian giant hornets that construct their nests in trees, the *veiio* build theirs in the bushes of thatch grass, and that's where I saw them as a young girl. (The big wasp gets its name from the thatch grass itself, called *veiio*.) The nests were as large as water buckets that the Tsou people used in the past. Sometimes, they were so large that thatch bushes couldn't cover them completely. Sometimes, you would find the hives built underground. The Great Creator's wonders!

The big wasps, although large in size, are not as aggressive as giant hornets (*zeoiu*). They won't attack people unless provoked. I've never heard of anyone being stung by big wasps. Tsou people have an easy first aid for bee stings: use urine that is still warm to spread over the stung area. Alternatively, one could apply ginger roots or the tender leaves of kudzu to the affected area.

Finding and Harvesting Hives and Nests

Whether it was giant hornets or big wasps, when their larvae were still white in color, they tasted the best. The Tsou people knew very well the best time to harvest them: It was too early when the larvae were still transparent; it was too late when they turned to imagoes (insects in their sexually mature adult state). Based on the size and the color of a hive or nest, one could judge the best time.

Bees are diurnal insects, therefore the best time to harvest their hives was at night, at a time when they were not as aggressive. Before flashlights were available, we carried one or two torches, and would slowly and quietly approach the hive. In other words, we'd conduct a surprise assault, guerrilla style, so that the bees wouldn't be agitated and come out to attack us. If they did, we could be stung and go home empty-handed.

The giant hornets built their nests on tree branches. Upon arriving in the woods, we'd quickly light the torches and position them by the entrance to the nests. Disturbed and scared, the hornets would rush out; some of them would escape, others would burn alive. If they attempted to attack us, we'd chase them away with the torch. The ones that escaped would find a new spot to build another nest, so that they could continue their new lives. Once the situation was safe, an able body would climb the tree, sever the nest, and hand it over to a team member under the tree.

To harvest larvae from a bee hive, the Tsou people normally removed the outer layer of a beehive first, then put the inside layers of the combs in a steamer until the larvae were fully steamed. We'd then remove the larvae one at a time from the comb and put them on a plate. Sprinkle some salt on them and they are ready for serving. Live larvae can also be fried.

Tsou people are good at sharing. Customarily, the person who discovered a beehive would put out a sign to indicate that a hive had been found, so that other people would know that it belonged to the finder. This sign was made by tying a blade of silver grass to the tip of a wooden stick that was pointed in the direction of the beehive. When it was time for harvesting, the finder would notify the neighbors and they would all go remove the hive together. On the trip to the hive and back home again, and while the larvae were being steamed, everyone took the opportunity to chat, gossip, and renew their relationships!

The larvae were divided up into equal portions for each of the participating families; the finder also received the same amount, no more no less. The message here was: The delicacy was a blessed gift from Mother Nature; it was not farm raised or cultivated by the finder or other humans. Even though larvae were nothing out of the ordinary, when the Tsou left for home, they walked with a heart as warm as torches. That's because they'd had a wonderful get-together with their friends, and would soon have a rare delicacy to share and enjoy!

Little Ground Bees

When I was in the primary school, kids from the fifth district and from the sixth district lined up on the same route to the school in two separate processions. It took about one hour for the kids from the fifth district, of which I was a member, to walk to the school. It was even farther away for the kids of the sixth district; for example, the Yangs' house was about seven or eight kilometers farther from my house. The Yangs left home more than one hour earlier than we kids from the fifth district. For the younger kids, the trip would be more than two hours! The team captains, who were students of upper classes, had to be patient and maintain a strong sense of responsibility. To begin a school day, we all had to be up early in the morning. Our breakfasts, of little substance to begin with, would dissipate in little more than one hour of walking—young growing bodies digested and absorbed food fast! With this in mind, while walking to and from the school, not only did we need to watch out for stones which could trip us, but we also had to keep our eyes peeled for things that might be edible, such as wild strawberries, passion fruits, and rarely-found snow-white mountain tea seeds that appeared by the road in late spring and early summer. Whatever we found would be shared by all.

One day, a sharp-eyed, big male student noticed a few small unknown bees flying to the underside of a large rock by the road. He followed the bees, as did the rest of the procession. That male student dug into the hole where the bees had disappeared. He then used a blade of bamboo to dig farther. We had no idea what he was doing. Finally, he dug out something yellow, about the size of his palm, and began to eat it. What was *that*? Every one of us rushed up to get a share and taste it; I was no exception. It was almost like cooked egg yolk, soft and fluffy, a little sweet and with a hint of sourness—rather tasty! We all wondered what type of bee this was. No one knew. An excited discussion erupted to name the bees. Because these bees built nests in the ground, we finally decided to call them "little ground bees." We all agreed that the term was well conceived and felt very satisfied about it!

To protect the interests of each one of us, we had agreed that none of the fifth and sixth district students should ever dig a nest alone. Because of the delay caused by the "little ground bees" episode, the procession captain yelled loudly: "Move fast or we will be late!" All of us, old or young, walked fast on the steep trail; soon we were breathing rapidly, our faces warm and flushed by our exertions. No one wanted to be late and be punished by being spanked, or made to stand facing a wall. Later, the agreement was broken by a selfish, impatient individual who, when no one was around, dug the nest before it was big enough. This caused everyone else to be upset for not having a share of the royal jelly. The little ground bees must also have been so fed up by the thoughtless kid—and other greedy kids as well—that they left altogether! That was the only time that I had ever tasted the little ground bees' very "royal" royal jelly.

Building a House

While the family members were chatting, gathered around a fire, Father announced passionately: "The kids are growing up; we need a bigger house!" Upon hearing this I asked, as if I were electrically shocked with excitement, "Is it true? What kind of a house?"

That was during summer break when I was in the second grade. In those days, in order to save on the use of kerosene, which we purchased from afar and carried home with great effort, we lit our lamps only when we kids were doing homework or when guests were visiting. After sunset, all of the familial activities were carried out around a large fire; dried bamboo stems and wood were free and abundant on our own land. Father would weave bamboo and rattan baskets, and use hemp fibers to make ropes or tote bags. We kids would assist Mother in shelling peas, and polishing rice with a traditional stone mortar and pestle. Anything and everything was done by the fire, be it chatting, listening to stories from the adults, discussing unusual or trivial events that had happened to the villagers, or receiving reprimands. These were very intimate times, a chance for the family members of all generations to share their joys and sadness. It was only when it was time to go to bed that we lit the kerosene lamps, which shed a dim light showing the way to the bedroom. Once in the bed, we extinguished the light.

Why was I so excited when I heard Father's announcement? To be true, it was because of my childhood memory of houses. When I was a kid, my family's house was a few kilometers away from the village. The houses in the village were different from ours. The outer walls of their houses were covered with nailed-down wooden boards, and inside there were lumber "pillars," white walls, and glass doors and windows—all were beautiful looking! In contrast, our house, which was built by our grandfather, was constructed with bamboos, and so were the windows; when the windows were closed, no light could come into the house, blocking the precious sun from entering. What a pity! That memory from my childhood makes me value light shining into a house more than the house itself.

Naturally, I was very excited to hear that we would be building a new home. As a result, after moving in I was the most diligent family member when it came to keeping the house neat and clean. Even though the house was simple and not at all sophisticated, I used a cleaning device made of straws to scrub each and every bamboo pillar until it was totally spotless. I didn't have to worry about damaging the paint because there wasn't any!

Once we had decided to build a new house, Father, during his spare time, began clearing a piece of land and searching for rock to use for the foundation. In between farming activities, he would use a chisel to cut stone. In the tool basket that he shouldered were a new chisel and mallet, which he had recently made himself. Because tools constructed of iron would become dull after long use, Father would forge new ones by hand. He would often ask me to operate a bellows to keep charcoal flames red hot in the furnace. (Father, of course, produced the charcoal himself.) You would hear "*hu lu, hu lu*" sounds as the wind was pulled into the bellows. When the piece of iron was as red as the flaming charcoal, Father would hold a pair of iron pliers with his left hand and place the iron on an anvil. With his right hand, he would hold a palm hammer to strike the iron a few times, then bring the iron back to the stove to heat up again. This process went on continuously until he was happy with the forging. One might ask: Why let a young girl take up a task like mine, when she had strong and able brothers? Well, that was how my father was. He believed that in our "impoverished" state everyone should chip in to help with household work, be they male, female, grownups, or youngsters. The stronger ones would tackle the heavier work, the others the lighter chores. While my brothers would help Father with heavier work, operating the bellows was not a job so physically demanding that I, a little girl, couldn't handle it.

After Father found a large piece of rock suitable for building purposes (it normally would weigh a few tons), he would examine the grains that ran through the rock, and fracture the rock accordingly. For roughly every eight *tsuns* along the grain,[30] Father would chisel a hole about one *tsun* in diameter. The depth of a hole would depend on the size of the rock to be chipped off; for example, in the case of a piece weighing more than six or seven tons, a depth of more than 10 *tsuns* would be needed. Chiseling holes into a big rock was an extremely time-consuming task, and one that required much patience. A single strike into a rock usually yielded only a small amount of fine stone debris. While carving the holes, one also needed to remove that debris from time to time.

Once all the holes were made, an iron stick was placed in each. A heavy mallet weighing about five kilograms was used to strike each stick in sequence, a process that was repeated until a piece of rock began to break off. First, there'd be a cracking sound—*"Po!"*—that

---

30. A tsun *is a unit of measuring length used in Taiwan; one* tsun *is equal to 3.03cm.*

revealed the initial separation of a narrow section of rock from the whole. Then one used a long iron bar, like a crowbar, with the flat side inserted into the crack to gradually pry open the crack. While doing this, one inserted pebbles into the crack to fill up the gap; the gap would grow wider and wider until the piece of the rock was completely separated from the rest. This method was used to break a large chunk of rock into smaller chunks of a suitable size and shape. The surfaces of the chunks were smoothed out to make them look aesthetically pleasing. The finished rocks were then transported to the construction site for use in the building of the foundation.

Rattan was usually used by Father to fashion the handle of a mallet because rattan had greater elasticity than wood, which made the striking movement easier and more effective. In this regard the mallet was similar to the poles used in pole vaulting; today these are made of plastic fibers which provide better elasticity, enabling vaulters to jump higher than they ever did when using poles made of wood.

My father truly was an expert in chipping stones and puzzling the pieces together. Whenever anyone in the village wanted to build a house, they would come to him for the stone foundation work. Father was an artist too! When Taiwan was under Japan's occupation, the beautifully carved words on the monument of the village's elementary school, as well as the identifying plaque at the local police station were created by him. Later when these buildings were rebuilt, the carved signs were lost, apparently buried thoughtlessly with other debris. It was a big pity that I wasn't there at the time to save them.[31]

---

31. It is a tradition in Taiwan to erect a stone or cement plaque at the entrance of a school, university, or other facility to bear its name.

Based on the planned size and the layout of the rooms, the ground was dug and the stone foundation was laid down accordingly. After that, carpenters took over. To save money, building materials such as stones, bamboos, and lumber were collected from one's own land, which required considerable time and labor. Carpenters, however, were hired because their work required real professional skills.

Amazingly, a carpenter's blueprints were stored in his head. No plans were needed. And neither were nails! When the pieces of bamboo or wooden lumber were connected together, they always fit perfectly, without even a tiny problem. The common tools carpenters used were a chalk box, steel square, metric ruler, and a pencil that was usually kept behind the carpenter's ear. There was a chisel for wood work, several saws (including a large saw that cut lumber into square pieces or sliced it into boards), and hand saws for precision cuts. Since all the dimensions for doors, windows, pillars, and roof beams were in the carpenters' heads, all they needed were the materials. The carpenter who helped us was a neighbor who lived three to four kilometers away from our house. His daughter was my classmate. He sometimes brought her with him when he worked on our new house, so that the two of us could play together.

According to the government's regulations, pine trees grown on the reservation—land set aside for the aboriginal peoples— could not be harvested without a permit issued by the Ministry of Forestry. (The procedure to apply for a permit was very cumbersome; the applicant had to go through the local police station, village bureau, county bureau, and, finally, the Ministry of Forestry itself.) Father was very reluctant to deal with the government agencies, and he didn't want to apply for a permit whose process was so time consuming. Therefore, he harvested trees grown on our own land. The trees on our own land, however, were not as valuable as the pine and Hinoki Cypress that grew on the reservation land.

Before the carpenter completed his carpentry work, he would inform family members of the date that he intended to install the roof beams. Putting them up was a solemn event; all of the close relatives and neighbors (actually, the so-called neighbors lived kilometers away) were invited. During the installation everything was taken very seriously lest any mishaps occur. In observance of an old superstition, kids were kept quiet to prevent something "evil" from being accidentally spoken. Although the adults remained nervous until the roof beams were smoothly in place, the kids were already anxiously awaiting the next event, for reasons that soon will be obvious!

Mother would fill a round bamboo basket, or *kam'bua*, with *mochi* balls[32] and various kinds of homemade candies, and hand the basket to the carpenter. From his perch on the roof's ridge beam, he would say blessings for the family, then grab a bunch of goodies from the basket and throw them onto the ground. The kids would scurry about and scream excitedly while picking up the candies and *mochi* balls. Having grabbed all they could, each would count the number of items he or she had picked, and a winner would be declared. (Adults would join the activity too.) They would eat the *mochi* balls after the dirt was dusted off. In order to celebrate the successful beam installation, and also to show appreciation to the carpenter, Father would ask Mother to prepare wine and foods, and all of us would celebrate the occasion together.

---

32. A small, round-shaped sweet rice cake.

Because roofing was such a big endeavor, word would go out to all the villagers in order to enlist their help. It would take several dozen villagers to roof a house in one day. Normally, villagers would gladly volunteer. In the event someone could not, he would notify the owner of the house and ask to be excused. How available a person was when labor was needed would serve informally as a record of how helpful a person was in general. If a person was helpful most of the time, most villagers would be quick to help him when he was in need.

Other than government offices, which had tile roofs, villagers' houses were roofed with materials that were available locally; mostly we used Makino Bamboo (桂竹) for roofing because its fibers are dense, tough, and durable.

When villagers showed up on roofing day, the physically stronger ones would go straight to the forest to cut down bamboos. It was a demanding job because the land was so steep. They needed to pick bamboos that were strong and straight, usually about six meters long.[33] While in the forest they would strip everything from the culm. They needed to make sure that each culm's upper end fell in the direction opposite to that of the route back to the construction site, in order to make it easier for the volunteer worker hauling the load. There were two ways to haul bamboos: one, bundle them up and carry the entire bundle on the shoulder; two, bundle them up but have one bamboo sticking out. In the latter instance the worker would place this protruding culm on his shoulder and pull the entire bundle forward while its distant end remained on the ground.

---

33. *Bamboo is actually a grass, not a tree; the main stem is called a culm, which is the structure for the branches and leaves, and is the Tsou's primary building material.*

Transporting bamboos was a most physically demanding job. It might take more than one hour to get them from the bamboo forest to the construction site. Fortunately, our new house was built on our own land, and the forest was only about 20 minutes away. This meant that the workers could carry more bamboos, depending of course upon their physical strength, and as a result the construction work would proceed considerably faster.

Once at the construction site, the bamboos would be handled by the volunteers, who worked collectively as a team. The bamboo ends were trimmed neatly so that they would be equal in length, which was necessary for roofing. The bamboo culms would then be carefully split into two halves by the more experienced workers. The way a culm was split was to place a knife diametrically at the broader end of the bamboo and hammer the knife a few times until the bamboo began to split. The worker would then step on the end of one split half while the other half was lifted by hand. Voila! The entire bamboo culm would separate into two equal lengths! An experienced, strong worker could split open a six-meter-long culm into two perfect halves in a single breath. (Alas, if he failed, that piece of bamboo wouldn't be usable, and the effort of carrying it to the construction site would unfortunately be wasted.)

After splitting the culm, a worker would use a semi-circular, curved-shaped rasper, a kind of course file, to knock off the diaphragms at the nodes inside the bamboo culm. Then a notch of about 10 centimeters would be cut across at the center of the split and heated up.[34] While the notch area was still hot, the worker would hand the bamboo up to

---

34. *This was done to make the bamboo in that section more flexible and thus easier to bend.*

his co-workers on the roof; they would place the notch area above the ridge beam, then bend the two ends down so that one end formed the front eaves of the house and the other the back eaves. These bamboo halves would be tightly aligned next to each other. A bamboo half was then placed, with the hollow culm facing down, on top of two adjacent face-up culms so that they were intertwined. This process was repeated until the first layer was completed; the second layer was built in similar fashion.[35] Finally, sweet bamboo (麻竹)—with diameters as large as 30 centimeters—was used for the roof ridge. It was also split into halves with the node diaphragms knocked off and placed face down on the roof edge. Each half was fastened tightly with iron wires or hemp rope to prevent rain water from passing through the roof ridge and leaking into the house. And with that, the roofing job was completed!

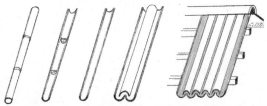

Illustration (drawn by the translator) of the roofing procedure (L - R). Sections of Makino Bamboo were cut and then split into perfect halves. The diaphragms inside were knocked off before the sections were used for roofing.

I should add that a roof had other uses too. Normally, the angle from the roof's ridge to the eaves was about 30 degrees. When needed, roof space could be used as a sun-baking place to dry such things as millet and tasty young bamboo shoots.

On roofing day, the hosts would treat the hungry and tired volunteer helpers well by serving them a sumptuous lunch and dinner. According

---

35. The author explained that about every ten years the second layer, or top layer, had to be replaced with a new layer of bamboo.

to Tsou custom, a bounteous amount of pork, chicken, fish, and vegetables was provided. Workers often would use the leaves of banana plants to wrap up some of the food to take with them when the job was done. They were concerned that since their stomachs were not accustomed to such lavish meals, they wouldn't eat as much as they'd like at the roof raising, and would be hungry for more later on when they got back home!

In the past, to prepare for the special feasts that were part of a major event such as a roofing, villagers would raise several pigs for the occasion—and save the money they would have spent had they purchased the pork. Because houses were scattered in the remote mountains and it could take two days to reach a slaughterhouse, villagers were allowed to slaughter the pigs themselves and without paying taxes, as long as they informed the local police station in advance. The kind-hearted villagers would give the police some pork in return as a show of appreciation.

The dinner was especially sumptuous! And they all celebrated with joy for having completed a major construction event! In addition to the pork, millet wine would be served for the drinkers. Today, soft drinks, along with goodies like candy, are made available for people who don't drink alcohol.

****

With the roofing out of the way, it was time to construct the walls. Makino Bamboos were split into long bands, or strips, which were used to pass through the horizontal slots that the carpenter had carved out earlier in the wooden studs, or interior upright support beams.

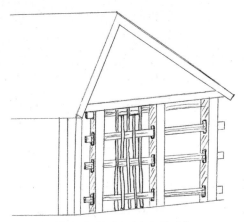

Thinner bamboo strips were used to weave the walls vertically between the studs. People normally did this type of work themselves, so it could take a substantial amount of time.

Once the weaving was completed, it was necessary to paste a mix of soil and water on the walls. Because

Illustration (drawn by the translator) of building a house wall using lumber pillars and bamboo strips.

the soil on our land wasn't sticky enough, we'd have to travel quite a distance to find suitable yellow soil and carry it home—a tough chore indeed. An alternative solution was to use the fibers from chopped dried hemp and mix them with soil to strengthen its cohesiveness. This way, after the soil paste had dried on the wall it wouldn't peel off easily.

Next, we'd apply white chalk to the wall. Actually, it wasn't too difficult a job, but ... . While I am writing the word "but," my heart suddenly sinks, my nose and throat stuff up, and my eyes tear because the very idea of this endeavor makes me appreciate the ability of human beings to realize their potential by overcoming incredible hardship.

How would I be able to adequately describe the heartfelt intentions and sacrifices made by my parents in providing their children a more comfortable living environment? Simply obtaining white chalk, for example, was an extremely difficult task! Because of our financial hardship, we needed to evaluate what was the least costly way to obtain the white chalk. If shipped by cargo train, it still would require of us a three-hour round trip to carry it to our construction site from the nearest train station. And the purchasing and shipping wouldn't be cheap! As there was no highway, we would have to carry it all on our backs. One afternoon, Father, our uncle, my elder brother, several villagers, and Mother left for Kong Tien (公田), the closest town that had chalk available; it was still several dozen kilometers away. I didn't know where they all stayed overnight. I remained at home to take care of my first-grade brother and two younger sisters (the younger one was only a little over a year old). It wasn't until early evening the following day did I see them coming home, exhausted. At least I had the dinner ready for them as requested by Mother beforehand!

The walls weren't done yet. The final task involved some kind of secretion from tree bark, which would be mixed with white chalk to increase its stickiness. We'd season the mixture for a period of time, stirring it occasionally while waiting for the soil on the walls to dry; only then could we apply white chalk on top of the soil layer. The thickness of the soil was a little over one centimeter, on both sides of the walls. A single centimeter, or less, was the best we could do because the chalk, as I've noted, was so difficult to obtain.

Once the walls were finished, we needed to build a stove-like cooking structure. We accomplished this by stacking rocks and filling the spaces between them with soil. Because tree debris was burned for cooking and the debris would generate a lot of ash, an iron grid was placed approximately 12 cm above ground level so that the ash could slip between grids and fall downward. This setup left enough space for a sufficient amount of air to enter the stove from beneath the grid, which would ensure proper burning. Because there were usually two ovens in a single stove, enough smoke would be generated to require a chimney. We'd have to build that too. A cover was installed on top of it to prevent rain water from pouring down and onto the ovens. A space was left between the chimney and its cover to allow smoke to escape.

Last but not least was the floor surface inside the house. Given that we lacked the financial resources to pave the floor with costly cement, we'd loosen up the dirt inside the house and spray it with water until it became saturated. We, the family members, would then stomp on it until the dirt became sticky. We used bamboos to smooth out the ground, and a wooden tool designed specifically for leveling dirt floors. There was a handle at one end of this tool that was meant to be grasped by both hands; at the other end was a wide, thin, and flat board. The worker would forcefully strike the board against the floor to flatten and compact the dirt. One had to make sure that equal force was exerted each time the board hit the ground, otherwise the dirt wouldn't be compressed evenly. The process was repeated through-out the entire house—all the rooms, walkways, etc. After living in a house like ours for a while, the floors would become loosened and dust would fly. Thus, it was necessary to re-do the floors every few years.

A seemingly endless number of days later, the house was finally ready to be occupied. What still excited me the most, looking back on it today, was that there were windows to let in sunlight—the inside was as bright as the outside! In the Tsou manner, a new house normally required a kind of trial run. This meant that the younger adults would live in it for a period of time, to see whether there were any bad omens or safety concerns. If everything was OK, the entire family would move in. Then it was time to warm the house, in a very special way: All the villagers would be invited over to help us celebrate—again!

3. Work

'Tis the Season to Harvest Palm Fiber Sheaths

My Second Aunt was sitting on a low stool, her body rhythmically moving forward and backward while sharpening a sickle on a grindstone. Her solemn face reminded me of her character: Whenever she was determined to do something for a cause, her face showed great solemnity. Second Aunt's stoic personality, exhibited in various facets of her life, had been shaped through long years of hardship. Actually, she was a very soft-spoken person; even when faced with an extremely intolerable circumstance, she would never raise her voice nor alter her tone. This was the steady, unflappable image I kept of her in my mind.

Next to her, on the ground, were several sharpened knives of various kinds; thicker ones for cutting trees, thinner ones for cutting grass, and a special square knife to remove the brown protective sheath-like covering found over new palm leafs. The blade of the latter knife was about five *tsun* in length, four *tsun* in width.[36] The handle of the palm fiber's knife was cast as one piece along with the knife blade, unlike knives that had separate wooden handles. Also, the size of the handle where the thumb and the index finger joined was smaller and gradually became thicker toward where the little finger held the handle— a design for the special purpose of harvesting palm fiber sheaths that

---

36. A tsun (寸) *is equivalent to 3.03 cm. By comparison, an inch equals 2.54 cm.*

required uniquely different cutting movements.

Long before my summer break, Second Aunt had asked me to go with her to harvest palm fiber sheaths in the remote mountains. I had been helping her during winter or summer school breaks (with my parents' permission) since I was in the third grade.

Before I continue, some background on my remarkable aunt is in order. She became a widow before she turned 30, and raised her two sons by herself. In our remote village, where educational endeavors were not common, her boys were academically outstanding: They both passed the entrance exams for admittance to the Special Normal Education Program at the Tai-Chung Normal School. The program was founded by the government of the Republic of China in those early days of the 1950s, to train teachers for the educationally backward and remote villages. Even though their tuition was waived, the living expenses at the Normal School had to be borne by trainees themselves.

That wasn't all. At that time, transportation was a big hassle. It took two days to travel from our village to Tai-Chung City, where the school was located. In order to avoid additional expenditures for travel and hotel accommodations, the students could only return home when the school semester was over. Second Aunt would try to have saved enough money for one semester to give to her sons when they came home for a visit; if she hadn't, she would continue to save, and send the money to them when they were back at school. She had to work doubly hard to support her boys—even doing things such as sharpening knives! It showed how much a widowed woman living under impoverished circumstances had to sacrifice for her children.[37]

In the early days, when I was a child living in our remote, isolated village, families were busy working just to provide everyone with three meals each day, let alone anything else. Despite passage of a compulsory education law that required every child to complete primary school, it remained rare for a student to go on to higher education; very few families could afford to pay for their children to study in the cities. Besides, the kids had to be very competent to be able to pass the entrance exams. At that time, only four or five kids from our village could do that—and Aunt's two sons were among them. Second Aunt had the foresight to know that for her sons to create a better future for themselves, they needed to pursue higher education at a respected out-of-town institution such as the Tai-Chung Normal School.

Prior to the advent of plastic materials, some villagers deemed the village's climate suitable for growing palm trees, and encouraged their neighbors to do so. Byproducts from the palm trees, like palm fiber, could be used to make brushes, brooms, and palm rain capes; these items could be found in virtually every household. It would take a good five years before the palm fibers were mature enough for harvesting, however. During that time the soil around the palm trees required annual weeding; there were also the demands of land clearance, and maintenance. Right now, though, Aunt's palm trees were ready for her to use to raise some

---

37. *Second Aunt's unflagging spirit and work ethic did not go unnoticed. She was twice awarded the Excellent Mother Award, bestowed upon her by the Taiwanese Government through a program called "Model Mothers," established to honor mothers who excelled at producing well behaved and high performing children. A deserving mother was first recommended by her village head to a county official, and then to the government for an award that usually included a plaque and sometimes money.*

money for her sons. The timing might have been Aunt's plan all along!

Second Aunt's palm tree farm was deep in the mountains; on foot it took one to two hours, each way. In order to save time spent walking to and from the farm, she figured that if we simply stayed there it would take only about one week to harvest the palms. So at home we gathered together everything we would need to bring with us: tools, blankets, mat sheets, pots, rice, salt, salted meat, salted fish, etc. The most important thing to remember to bring was matches. As long as matches were available, there were always wild vegetables in the mountains that could be cooked for food. Also, the palm trees that had not grown in a normal, healthy fashion could be cut down and their young growth cooked with meat, just like villagers nowadays cook the new growth of areca palms as food.

Because harvesting palm trees was a once-a-year event, there were no permanent shelters at the palm tree farms as there were by rice fields, which were frequented more often. Therefore, upon their arrival at a palm farm workers—like us!—would clear a piece of land by a creek, use wood-cutting knives to cut down arm-sized trees for building a shelter, and pick some rattan stems to function as nails to hold the structure together. Thatch grass was collected for use as roofing and as walls. At a corner inside the shelter, a thick layer of grass would be laid down and covered with a mat sheet. Ta-da! A soft and comfortable bed was thus ready for use. It took only about an hour for the two of us to complete all of these chores.

I cut a section of sweet bamboo (麻竹) three to four feet long, leaving the diaphragm at the end of the section. I knocked off a second diaphragm at the center of the section with a wooden stick. Voila! A piece of bamboo to use as a container to carry the water.

I found three pieces of rock and erected them in a formation so that a fire could be lit and a pot rested on them to boil water, using dried wood that I'd found nearby. We were both quite thirsty, having had nothing to drink since we left the house before dawn several hours ago. Here in this remote mountain region, it wasn't easy to enjoy many creature comforts, or ensure personal hygiene; the least we could do was exercise enough common sense to boil the water before drinking it. We knew that some people drank water straight from the streams, without knowing whether or not it contained leech larvae. Once this larvae feeds on human blood, it can multiply in the human body. I heard of a classmate who often suffered from nose bleeds, and over time became physically weaker. Upon examination, a doctor discovered several big fat larvae in her nostril, feeding on her blood. How disgusting!

Our water break over, Aunt lost no more time and got to work. Her inexhaustible energy and the swift movements of her hands and feet were the result of years of hard labor coupled with an iron will.

I should add here that there were several reasons why my parents allowed me to accompany Second Aunt to the mountains. First, if something happened to her, there would be no one around to assist. Second, I had always been a nice, helpful kid, and was capable of doing things. To show her gratitude, when I was younger Aunt would make me a floral dress; when I was older she would offer me money.

Once the water had boiled, I covered the burned wood with ash to prevent it from dying out and so that it could be lit again later when needed. This was easy: just remove the ash, add additional dried leaves or wood sticks, blow air at the pile—and it would catch fire again. In those years when we had a meager supply of material things, even one match was very precious. Without having matches in the remote mountains, one not only couldn't cook food, but worse, could become sick from the cold; at the very least you could not sleep comfortably. Up here, the temperature could drop to the teens (Celsius) at night, even in the summer.

With clean water in hand, I went to where Aunt was working and asked her to take another break and have a drink. After she resumed her work, I stayed next to her and got to work myself. Carrying as much as I could manage, I neatly stacked the palm sheaths she had cut off, by the side of the temporary shelter we had built. In case of rain, they would be covered with large taro leaves. If they became wet they wouldn't sell for a good price.

At some time close to noon, judging by the position of the sun, I rinsed a small amount of rice, cut some yams, and cooked them together. Because there was no cutting board or yam peeler in the wild, I had to use the "hob" cutting method to slice the yams, which requires some skill. Here's how: Hold a yam loosely in your left hand, and decide roughly how big you would like each piece to be. While controlling the amount of force to strike the yam at the correct angle, hold the knife there and push its blade outward to break off the piece of yam and allow it to fall into a pot. Continue this process with your left thumb rotating the yam in your left hand until the entire yam is cut into small pieces. Be careful to control the force precisely lest the knife cut your hand. Cooking rice with dry wood debris also required skill. Once the water was boiling, I spread the wood sticks to lessen the intensity of the fire, so that I didn't burn the rice. Once the rice was cooked, I prepared a pot of vegetable stew, and invited Aunt for a meal before she went back to work—yet again. These chores were what I could accomplish when I was smaller; once I was around twelve, I learned how to harvest palm sheaths.

At work, we always carried a sickle to cut grass. We carried it inside a simply-made knife scabbard, and tied the scabbard to the waist. Before we harvested palm sheaths, we cut the outstretched petiole, or leafstalk, first, and then using the thumb and the index finger, separated the palm sheath from the remaining petiole with the sickle. After cutting off the remaining petiole and discarding it, we detached the sheath from the palm trunk along the circular knot structure line. During this process, we would embrace the trunk, with our head on its right side while using the left hand to detach the sheath. Finally, we used the right thumb and index finger to forcefully cut off the last segment of the sheath—about a foot long— from the trunk. For each palm tree, we could harvest just three or four pieces of sheath, since any more might harm the tree.

The author cutting a fiber sheath off a palm tree.

A palm fiber sheath that is used for making rain caps, brooms, and brushes.

That day, we worked until dusk, and cooked our dinner together. Afterwards, Aunt sharpened the knives we had used. Then we went to the creek for a quick sponge bath. While the fire was still radiating rays of warmth, and after a long day of hard work, we shared a blanket and quickly fell asleep. At night, we were awakened once in a while by loud sounds from nocturnal animals, prompting Aunt to get up and add wood to the fire. While some of the animal sounds made us feel a bit uneasy, we were so tired we would quickly fall asleep again.

Because we went to bed early the night before, I awoke early (we mountain workers were used to getting up early anyway), but not as early as Aunt, who had prepared breakfast before dawn. After eating, we got right to work. We spent six days like this at the palm farm.

A little past seven in the morning of the seventh day, six or seven men and women arrived at the farm, as per the arrangement Aunt had made with them beforehand. After a short rest, they all began to work, knowing that the earlier they started, the sooner they could go back home.

They worked hard, chatting and teasing one another to make the atmosphere enjoyable. Sometimes one would sing songs and the others would sing along. They sang Tsou folk songs, theme songs from Japanese movies, and even Mandarin pop songs learned from 78 rpm long-playing records. At the time, only two families in our village owned a hand-powered phonograph.[38] The normally very quiet and remote mountains suddenly became bustling. This helped too with the

---

38. *Because Taiwan was a colony of Japan from 1895 to 1945, Japanese songs became popular during that era. The Republic of China took over Taiwan from Japan in 1945, after Japan surrendered to the Allied forces. Mandarin was then used by the government as the official language.*

loneliness Aunt and I had experienced over the past six days.

At noontime, Aunt asked me to cook more rice for the helpers, along with all of the salted pork and dried fish that had been reserved for them, even though they had each brought their own lunch box. For these workers, this apparently wouldn't be enough food! Thanks to a supplemental "hot from the oven" meal, they were extremely contented and worked really hard in the afternoon. By around four o'clock, they had finished the primary tasks.

They gathered the palm fiber sheaths into bundles and, each carrying what they could, proceeded back to the village. When I was smaller, I would carry a sleeping mat, blanket, and all of the knives, pots, and pans in a basket. The road from the remote mountains back to the village was winding and treacherous, especially for team members loaded with palm sheaths twice the size of their bodies. They walked at a snail-like pace, one small step at a time lest the heavy load on their back shift its center of gravity, making them lose their balance and fall down with it.

By the time we arrived at the village it was almost dark, and everyone was tired. But no one complained! During these tough economic times, exhaustion from physically demanding work was common; it was really a way of life. Nobody ever used the word "exhaustion," they simply went to bed early, got a good rest, woke up early, and started all over again.

Just because all of the harvested palm sheaths were carried home didn't mean that was the end of the job. It would take three or four sunny days to dry the sheaths and wrap them up. The latter process required certain skills. You placed the best quality sheath on the ground first, and the second one to overlap it by a half sheath on one side. This was done with five to six sheaths in a row. You followed the same procedure for the second row, which was placed one third lower than the first, using one fewer sheath per row. Repeat this for about five rows, then roll the whole thing up. You started rolling from one side, sometimes using your knees to assure a precision like that required when rolling Japanese sushi. Then you tied up the roll, about four feet high, with palm leaves or miscanthus grass. Finally, you tied five to seven rolls together to make a bundle.

The next step was to inquire about the current market price. Some businessmen from the plains would come to the palm-sheath maker in order to procure their product.[39] As long as we didn't borrow money in advance from a particular businessman, we could always take our time and wait for a better offer. If we had borrowed in advance, we would lose the opportunity to bargain with other buyers for a higher price.

That year, Second Aunt was fortunate to receive a good bargain offer, so that not only did my two cousins have enough money for the entire semester, there was enough left to enable Aunt to purchase what she needed for the household. When the semester was over, the eldest cousin even brought home what was the first (and only) camera in our village. It was really an eye-opening experience for the villagers to see such a novel device, and they lined up to take a photo with his camera.

---

39. *Most Tsou, and other indigenous people, lived, then as now, in the mountain regions. Others, such as the non-aboriginal Han and "business" people, continue to live in the plains where the land is mostly flat.*

Millet Farming

Preparing the Land

M illet (*ton'u*) has long been the Tsou people's staple food. When the supreme god Amo Hamo created the Tsou people on Mt. Jade, he dispatched the Goddess Millet (*nivunu*) to distribute millet seeds and the seeds of other traditional crops to the people and teach them how to cultivate and use them. Therefore, in traditional folklore, people treated millet with great respect. This was true for each and every stage of farming—from seeding, harvesting, and storage to consumption—because millet was so essential to the lives and welfare of the people. Millet was all the more important since the Tsou were not aware of the existence of rice until much later, when they came in contact with the Han people.[40]

Historically, the Tsou lived in the mountains. They had tremendous respect for nature, its power and majesty, and were humbled by how small and insignificant humans seemed in comparison. They knew that millet, that life-sustaining, golden-colored grain, was a precious gift from nature and not very easy to obtain. They treated each step of the process, from preparing the land for planting to harvesting the bounty, with great care and solemnity.

---

40. *The Han emigrated to Taiwan over the past several centuries only. The majority of them are of ethnic-Chinese descent.*

Traditionally, before the family elders would pick out a farming location, they would request in dreams their gods' approval; if the first location didn't pass muster, the elders would pick another location, and so on, until a final approval was granted.

Throughout their history, the Tsou had never used a calendar. All farming activities were instead conducted according to the seasonal cycles of nature. For example, when certain trees blossomed, it was time to perform certain farming activities. Another example: The first full moon following the budding of certain trees would mark the beginning of the farming season. The actual farming of crops, including crop selection of types of beans and grains, would be done in accordance with the subsequent stages of the moon. This same calendar-free method was followed for hunting and fishing as well. Everything had to follow nature's cycles, and be in harmony with nature. This was Tsou wisdom for survival. The Tsou could be said to be the people who for guidance in farming looked up to the "sky."[41]

In their daily lives, the Tsou people regularly looked up the stars. Being natural astronomers, they realized how insignificant they were in comparison with nature (of which the stars of course were a part), which provided them with everything they needed. This resulted in a very powerful feeling not just of respect for but submission to nature; the notion of literally "conquering nature" never entered their minds.

Once a location had been selected for farming millet—after the tender yellow flowers of the Taiwanese rain trees turned into red

---

41. The word "sky" is a literal translation from the Chinese character "天." Taken broadly it encompasses such things as the seasons, climate, weather conditions, and nature itself.

fruits and then into the color of coffee—the Tsou would walk to the proposed site armed with a variety of knives, each designed for a different task; these included thick knives to cut trees, and sickle knives to cut grass and wild vines. Men and women, lined up in a row, energetically strode into a wilderness of thick grass, kudzu vines, and trees. Once the land clearing began, all one heard were the sounds of grass-cutting and the louder noise of trees crashing down. One might occasionally hear faint conversations among workers who remained fairly hidden from one another by trees and the dense, tangled foliage.

In keeping with the Tsou's closeness to and respect for nature— a tradition that was thousands of years old—they would cultivate a piece of land just large enough to yield enough millet for their needs during the upcoming year. They would never cultivate out of greed more land than was actually needed—an approach that resulted in minimal impact upon this precious resource.

Prior to burning the debris left from the trees and grass they had cut down, they would clear a swath of at least ten feet surrounding the open plot to serve as a safety zone, so that fire wouldn't pass that zone and spread to the adjacent land. Where the land was relatively steep, the width of the swath above and below the cleared land would be made even wider. Any dried debris that could easily catch fire would be removed from the swath.

Once the swath was completed, an application was filed with the local police authority for a permit allowing the farmers, on a certain date only, to torch the land. November was the best time. By then the cut trees and grass had nearly dried, and the weather was cooling down. The sweet-bamboo sections utilized for water-carrying were made ready in case there was an uncontrollable fire—the worst thing that could happen when torching cleared land. For this the neighbors' assistance was needed. Everyone carried two long bamboo sections, and distributed them along the corridor swath. Normally, the burning was done at night, so that even the smallest escaped fire could be noticed and extinguished immediately.

There was this, too: The local policeman could see the fire in the dark, and knew who was burning the field based on permit application records. The policeman wouldn't feel confident in heading home for bed until the entire fire was dead. The next day the farmers would clear away any tree debris that had not completely burned; they would cut these pieces into short sticks, and carry some home to use as firewood.

Sowing Seeds

By mid-December, activity of a different sort could be seen on the cleared field, with the family elder busy sowing millet seeds and uttering prayers at the same time. Only skilled farmers did the sowing. The less skilled might spread the seed unevenly, so that upon germination they sprouted a clump here or a clump there, preventing healthy and optimal growth over the entire field.

Our millet fields normally were sited on land that was stony and had a rather steep slope, which made it difficult to use regular hoes for cultivation. No matter how far technology had progressed, it was still better to use the homemade hand adze called *tu'u.* This was an iron plate about eight inches to one foot long and one to two inches wide, with one end flat and wide and the other end narrow. It also featured a hook. For this part, the farmers would search for something appropriate and "ready made." Most desirable was a hard-wood branch from a tree such as an elm, guava, or tea oil camellia. A branch hook of around 40 degrees was considered ideal. It was necessary that the longer arm of the hook be small enough for a person to hold it with one hand; this arm was trimmed into a rectangular shape with a slight curvature. The iron plate was tied to the shorter arm of the hook with a long rattan string, using granny knots (we used this type of binding knot to secure a rope or line around an object). One end of the rattan string was tied to the longer arm of the hook and the other end was pulled back to tie with this end of the rattan string, once the iron plate was securely attached to the shorter arm.

With the adze in one hand, a farmer could use his other hand to hold a *tu'u* in order to remove weeds.[42] Just because a section of land had been burned didn't mean there weren't still weed roots in the ground. The silver grass root, in particular, grew in huge clusters and required much force to remove; if left alone, by spring they would emerge and hinder the growth of the tiny, germinating millet seedlings.

After the land was torched and before the millet seeds were sowed, if there had been no rains and the cleared land remained dried and dusty, workers who had been in the field the entire day might laugh and tease one another, saying: "Ha, you look like the dark-skinned person in the toothpaste ads!"[43] At some point, when the tribal people had learned more about the continent of Africa and some of its people, they might instead say jokingly to each other: "Mister Ambassador,

---

42. *The use of a hoe would require both hands.*
43. *In Taiwan, at the time, there was a well known toothpaste brand called* Darkie Toothpaste *(黑人牙膏). Depicted on the toothpaste tube was a handsome, dark-skinned man's face with a big smile, to highlight his pure white teeth.*

which country in Africa are you from?" A typical response would be, that he was from such-and-such country! Others who were not as knowledgeable about Africa would come up with a bogus country name and cause a big laughter among the crowd. Teasing each other like this made everyone relaxed after a long day of hard work.

Still, why *this* particular subject area for our joking and teasing? It was because our people, compared with other tribes, tended to have a darker skin. Couple that with the dry, black dust from burning the miscanthus grass, which was stirred up by workers' hoes and landing everywhere on our bodies: hands, face, feet, inside our clothes, and even our veiled hair. When we looked at each other, all we could see were two big eyes and bright white teeth. This of course closely resembled the dark-skinned person on the *Darkie Toothpaste* packages. And *that* was the reason why we found it so funny!

Cultivating a dry land which was usually far away from water sources would require workers to bring their own water for drinking. What to do with dirty hands when it was lunch time? Not much. Hygiene in the remote mountain region was beyond our control. If they carried chopsticks or spoons, workers could use those; if they forgot to bring them, they could chop a small twig and skin it or cut a section of bamboo to make instant chopsticks.

Weeding

The earliest time to sow millet was in December, and the latest, no later than mid-January. The timing depended on the altitude of the land and whether the slope was facing or away from the direction of the sun. Once sowed, the tiny but precious millet seeds would await the arrival of spring rains, so they could then germinate and grow. Nearly invisible on the ground and covered by spring mist, the tender new green buds, full of living energy, were such a sight to behold!

Once the millet had grown to three or four inches in height, it was time for the first weeding. The ash left over from the wild grass fires was the best fertilizer for the young millet seedlings; alas, it was also the best fertilizer for the weeds. Weeds always grew faster and more lustrous than millet did.

Weeding on a very steeply situated and densely seeded millet farm required the climbing skills of a goat. Without such agility, one could inadvertently step on and destroy the tiny, newly germinated seedlings. Worse yet, if one moved too abruptly, one could slip on the loose dirt and fall down the slope, not only damaging the tiny little plants, but also hurting him- or herself. That would be a pity! It was why we often heard elder workers telling the inexperienced younger ones: "Walk carefully with light steps, with light steps. Don't step heavily like cows do." Millet fields normally required weeding three times per crop. Thinning was also necessary, at the time of the first weeding, to avoid over-crowding of the seedlings and assure a healthy growth.

Wars Between Farmers and Birds

When millet plants began to blossom, it was very important to chase away the birds, because they loved millet as much as the Tsou people did themselves. When I traveled to the plains as a young mountain girl, it made me envious to see that only a few straw scarecrows —not farmers!—were needed to keep birds away from the many acres of rice fields. Here in the mountains, however, the vast woods were home to many birds, and the small piece of rice field hidden nearby was what the Tsou people needed to survive; unfortunately, their field was never hidden from the birds, for whom our crops were paradise. Therefore, for usually the months of May and June—the time rice and millet were beginning to blossom—the normally peaceful coexistence between birds and humans turned into outright warfare. After the harvest, however, that peaceful coexistence resumed and birds and humans returned to their own daily activities, with no interference from or animosity toward one another.

As the proverb says, "The early bird gets the worm." In this case, the bird not only gets the worm, but the millet as well! As soon as the sky began to show its dim light in the early dawn, the birds would start to fly to the farms for their breakfast. To chase them away, farmers, like the firefighters watching over the burning fields at night, needed to rush to the farm early in the morning while it was still dark. If the birds would only prey on fully mature grains, the farmers would feel all right about sharing with them—because the birds could only eat so much before their stomachs were full! Alas, they preferred to eat the not-yet-mature grains, those that were still at the stage of being juicy and sweet, with white grain milk inside. Birds of all types—sparrows, white and black sparrows—flew to the farms in droves and broke into the needle-head sized grains for the milk inside. Worse, they didn't do so grain by grain, but, rather, by the mouthful, while at the same time discharging feces. The speed of their destruction to millet and rice farms was beyond description.

If the bird chasers relaxed their guard for just a brief moment, those so-called commando birds would dive-bomb a millet farm and devour the millet grains very swiftly indeed. They seemed to actually enjoy what they were doing, happily chattering to each other, excited by not just the food but the fun of it all! Unless they were chased away, they would stay in the field all day long, eating and playing, before finally returning to the woods for a rest. Then they would invade the millet field once again, this time before dawn. It didn't take too many days before the millet field was totally eaten up.

When rice or millet ears matured, the stalks would bow under the weight of full, ripe grains. However, if not-yet-ripe grains were pecked by birds and therefore damaged the stalks would remain upright, with the grains inside hollowed out. As a result, a farmer's year-long dream of enjoying a good harvest would not be realized. In traditional Tsou culture, millet was cultivated to not only feed the Tsou, but also played a critical role in their annual religious harvest festival. If a family didn't have a good harvest, they would be looked down upon and labeled as lazy people, unless the poor harvest was shown to be caused by natural disasters. Birds didn't count.

To chase away birds from a tiny piece of millet farm located within a vast expanse of forest was a fatiguing job, even if guarded by three or four people. The ancestors of the Tsou people came up with an idea that made use of locally available materials. They would take a section of bamboo and split it open to about three quarters of the total length, and leave the remaining one quarter intact. Then they'd erect the bamboo along the border of the millet farm. A rattan strap was tied to the top end of one of the halves, and the other end of the strap was pulled over and tied to a post by a worker's shack. When a worker pulled the strap and released it right away, the two halves of the bamboo would strike against each other and produce a big noise— *Po! Po!*—loud enough to scare away the invaders. If shorter, dried bamboo halves were tied to the top of the bamboo section, the noise it produced would be even louder and more dramatic. If many such devices were erected at the middle or peripherals of the farm, it would only take one person to keep the birds at bay.

The Tsou also employed a hand-held bamboo device that could be carried. To make this they would cut a section of bamboo that consisted of two culms, which each contained the nodes at both ends. The sides of the culms were trimmed smooth so that it would be easier and more comfortable for a hand to hold the stick. Lastly, they'd split the bamboo all the way from the other end, including the diaphragm between the two culms. To stay awake, a farmer ran around the millet field while carrying the device, to check whether there were sneaky birds lurking around. He would yell loudly while simultaneously vibrating the device to make that *Po! Po!* noise to frighten the birds.

Regardless of whether it was a rice field or a millet field, when you chased birds away from your farm, they would often fly right onto neighboring fields. When that happened, it was important to notify your farmer neighbors so that they too could use the bird scaring devices to loudly shoo them all away. You can imagine how much chasing and scaring was going on in the mountains during this time!

During school breaks, when I was small, adults would assign me the bird-scaring chore. They said it was an easy job that didn't require much effort. That was definitely not the case.

To be effective, you had to be fully engaged from dawn to dusk, looking out in all directions and listening all of the time. When you saw birds or heard their sounds, you needed to trigger the devices and shout out loud from the bottom of your lungs. Such a task was not trivial for a little child! Since I was small and growing, I liked to eat. I could salivate just by visualizing in my mind the wild strawberries—ripe, full, and reddish—that grew in the vicinity of the farm. I'd just go for them, leaving other things behind no matter how important they might be.

I would wake up and leave the house before dawn. Once at the farm I was supposed to be constantly alert and, of course, constantly yelling. By noon, though, I was both tired and sleepy, and couldn't help dozing off. My *amo*, or father, knew me all too well; he would sometimes come from another farm and catch me by surprise. Noticing that I wasn't alert enough to keep the birds away, he would scold me for not doing my assigned job. Angrily, he would say to me, "You feed the birds with grains. Are you expecting to have a meal next?"

Harvesting

Before the millet had matured for harvesting, we began planting yams so that the land could be fully utilized. After the millet was harvested, the yam plants continued to absorb earth's nutrients, and would provide us side crops for another year.

When the golden-colored millet was ripe for harvesting, it was time to celebrate. The harvesting festival in a small village like ours was simple in scale—about the same as the festival for sowing, except here we held a bunch of golden millet stalks as part of our gratitude ceremony. Afterwards, the family elders would go to the farm to pick the best seeding grains for the next growing season. Then, the entire family, with much gratitude and enthusiasm, formally began the harvest.

The sickles we used to harvest millet were, naturally, made by ourselves. If necessary, we could also use scythes that normally were used for harvesting rice, though they were a little too large for millet. Everyone harvesting millet wore a rattan basket. All the fingers of the right hand, except the thumb, would hold a sickle. Using the right thumb to hold millet stalks at a point below one or two leaves, they'd push the stalks against the sickle blade and cut them. At the same time, the left hand took over the severed stalks while the right hand, which held a sickle, removed the one or two leaves from the stalks. Using this system the harvesters were able to cut stalks rather precisely into equal lengths, so that the severed stalks in the left hand would be about the same length. When the bundle in the left hand was large enough, the harvester would use prepared silver grass leaves to tie the bundle together, then throw it into the rattan basket. When the basket was full of bundles, the harvester would walk to a simple shed that was used for temporary storage; there, he, or she, would empty the basket and return with it to the field. At the end of the day, the farmers would carry all the harvested bundles collected in the shed to their homes.

The harvest season for millet was usually late June or early July— at a time when there was plenty of bright sun to dry it, since it was critical that millet be completely dry before storing. This final stage marked the end of about half a year's hard work.

In the past, the Tsou people's crop storage space at home was of various types. Some farmers used thinly-split bamboo strips to make huge baskets; some used large wooden boxes; and others stored millet on a bamboo platform above a fireplace. The latter was a good option. When there was fire in the fireplace, the heat could simultaneously keep the millet dry and prevent infestation by worms.

Harvest Festival

In the Large Communities—either my ancestors' traditional habitation place, which nowadays is called Dar Bang Tribe (達邦部落) or Ter Fu Ye Tribe (特富野部落)—celebrating the millet harvest was a solemn, complicated, and major event shared by the whole tribe. Many years ago, the entire harvest festival took about one month. It began with the cleansing ceremony. For two weeks, all participants, including those from the Small Communities, were supposed to refrain from eating things with a strong odor, such as fish, green onions, and leeks; they were to be solemnly respectful in what they said as well as in their general behavior; and were required to wash themselves and their daily used objects with silvery wormwood before taking part in the ceremonies. Thoughts and actions of the participants were guided by a respectful fear of their gods. They were expected to worship with gratitude, maintain respect for all life, and adhere to established societal ethics and orders.

Of course, not everything was observed in strict solemnity. While the festival proceedings were in progress, women would enthusiastically grind millet ahead of time for later ceremonial use; they would brew millet wine prior to the peak ceremonial days; and prepare gourmet food to entertain friends and relatives who would come to the festival from far and near.

The Taste of the First Pot-Cooked Millet from the Harvest

In those days, when there was no electricity for machines to remove husks from rice or millet, we used a mortar and pestle. It was no easy task to cook a pot of rice or millet back then, like it is today! First, we judged the amount of the millet needed for the meal by the amount of stalks, and put them above a fireplace until the husks were crispy, thus making them easier to be removed. When we ground the husks, we had to make sure the outer shell was completely removed, otherwise coarse debris would remain, which was not good for eating. There were two kinds of millet, similar to rice: one that was sticky, and one that wasn't. We used the sticky one to make millet cake.

When we cooked the first pot of millet or rice from the harvesting, all of the family members would gather together. To celebrate we would prepare more food than was actually needed. To ensure ourselves good fortune, we'd cook the first pot for dinner in an amount greater than could be consumed, so that there would be some left over—symbolic of an abundance of food for the entire year. Each time one of us would take some millet or rice out from the container, we would do it with a scoop, rather than turn the container upside down. Besides, before more rice or millet was ground, one should not use up all that remained in the container. We always left some to symbolize that there would be no shortage of grain.

So when we tasted that first meal from the new harvest, after nearly one year of hard labor, not only did we enjoy it with happiness and much respect and gratitude, but also with a solemn attitude.[44] Ah, the aroma of freshly cooked millet, permeating the air, becoming part of mind and body and shared by my family and me. This feeling, these sensations, even today I still remember vividly.

---

44. *In the culture of the mountain people, and in Taiwan in general, there is significant emphasis on "doing things with solemn attitude" to show respect—for nature, life, or for someone or something. Things here are done quietly, slowly, and usually with no smiling and a straight face.*

Labor Exchange Co-operative

In the old days, the Tsou people didn't have so-called currencies. Because most of the household items were made by ourselves, we exchanged with other families what we had for things we didn't have. This barter system depended on mutual trust. No one made money—there was no profit motive—and items were traded with faith in their quality. Ultimately, to obtain something, we had to work for it; no work, no "wealth" of desired goods.

Because no currency was used, labor needs would be met by fellow villagers, especially when a project required much labor and needed be done within a certain time period. These tasks included planting rice seedlings, harvesting rice crops, and building houses, etc. When assistance was needed, word was spread and the villagers would come quickly to help. If the work date was in conflict with that of another family, then the two families would consult with each other and resolve the conflict so that the villagers' labor force could be concentrated on just one family's work need at a time. While the villagers' help was totally voluntary, the host family was expected to prepare lunch and dinner to reward them for their day's labor. At the dinner, wine was served, and candies or equivalents were available for the persons who didn't drink, or for kids who came with their parents.

In addition to the types of work mentioned above, there was a lot of other, seemingly endless work required of a farmer's family.

For example, between planting rice seedlings and the rice harvest, weeding was required two or three times, and at least three times for millet farming. Additionally, there were crops of yam, bean, corn, and bamboo (actual forests in this case, which might consist of Makino, tortoise-shell, and sweet bamboo). Then there was bamboo shoot picking, to be taken care of according to seasons of the year, and the regular care of tung-oil trees. Some jobs required that multiple workers labor together at the same time. Doing so not only could speed up work completion, but also reduce loneliness and the feeling of isolation when they worked alone at their farmland in the remote mountains.

Carrying out these tasks was different than, say, the planting of rice seedlings, for which help on a large scale was required. Instead, a non-monetary system was created to exchange labor—the so-called Labor Exchange Co-op. During the Japanese occupation (from 1895 to 1945), it was called the Mutual Society, which nowadays is known at the Mutual Support Association. The difference between the Labor Exchange Co-op and the Mutual Support Association was this: Labor was exchanged in the former, while in the latter money was used to help those in financial need. Some ten people worked, at one time, to help families on a given day. Ten was about the right number, because to add more could concentrate the local workforce too much on a single family at the expense of others who perhaps needed to carry out season-sensitive work, be it weeds that were growing higher than the crops, or crops that couldn't wait much longer for harvesting.

It was necessary for the workers of this labor co-op system to have and carry their own hand tools and lunch boxes. Of course, if the hosts happened to have delicious foods or sweets on hand, some harvested fruits, or by chance had just slaughtered a pig, the farmers certainly wouldn't hide these treats, rather, they would gladly share them with the workers.

The Labor Exchange Co-op system was better organized among the immediate neighbors, enabling them to easily notify each other if there were changes of work location, or if the host family had to cancel the work schedule due to unexpected circumstances. In those days, when there were no modern electronic devices, there were two ways to communication to each other. The first entailed walking to a neighbor to speak in person with someone who might be one to two kilometers away. The second employed the "call-out-loud" method, a time- and energy-saving communication alternative. This approach was used for things ranging from personal messages to governmental notices (the latter would include community meetings, military training notices, vaccine notices, registered mail or express mail ready for pick-up by so-and-so at the postal office, etc.) A person who wanted to "call out loud" to someone would first find an optimal spot facing the intended recipient's house, so that the recipient of the message could hear the best; once it was noticed that someone was calling from afar, he or she would in turn find a good spot, such as on the top or the ridge of a nearby mountain, to listen.

This calling out across a valley was not an easy task. The person calling not only had to able to project his voice far and loud, but ensure that the recipient could understand what he was saying. The recipient needed to have good hearing, otherwise he might mishear the message and pass on faulty information that could result in serious problems. Fortunately, unlike today, people in the past were not overloaded with information that deadened their sensory organs; this meant that their hearing and cognitive abilities were well preserved and messages were rarely misheard.

As to the labor exchange need, it all depended on what was to be done. If the work involved something light, like weeding, then women workers could manage it. If it were something heavy, building terraced fields or cultivating sloped land for crops, male workers would be required. I should note that female workers would not be rejected by male workers just because they were physically weaker; a good example would be if families couldn't provide male workers due to sickness or the deaths of male members. Their family hardship would be understood and female workers would be accepted.

Occasionally, five or six unmarried young ladies of the neighboring families would form a labor exchange group, although it was different from the regular groups. When we joined the regular groups that had male members or married members, we, the unmarried young ladies, refrained from laughing openly when we heard sex jokes; we just pretended that we didn't understand them. But it was totally different when the group members consisted of only unmarried young ladies! In the remote mountains, where we were alone, we didn't have to behave lady-like; instead, we laughed out loud, and fearlessly announced our personal secrets—nothing was off limit. Even though the work was hard, we were happy girls.

Members of our young lady group wouldn't do physically demanding work, such as building terraced fields or clearing lands for farming. Rather, when we were freed up from work related to rice field and non-irrigated farmland, we collected fire wood, or pestled millet so that when it was time to cook rice, we didn't have to perform either of these tasks. The crisp sounds from pestle striking mortar gave us a feeling of abundance; we knew there would be no shortage of food stuffs. Although pestling rice required physical energy, we felt so happy and relaxed that we often sang songs or had small talks while we worked. After pestling and mortaring, we would pick and remove the grains whose bran wasn't totally polished. Sometimes, while we pestled and mortared rice, we baked yams as snacks. All of these activities were very enjoyable things to do.

I admired the patience and effort of a member of our group, named Chuang, for the way she took care of her skin. Most of us would just wear a hat made of bamboo leaves to protect us from the strong sunlight. Chuang, however, would put a flower-patterned square kerchief under the hat, and wear gloves and protective sleeves. Her legs were also covered with leg wrappings, called *kiahang*, that were used by Japanese workers. Not only that, she would place newly grown and tender banana leaves between her skin and the hat, gloves, sleeves, and leg wrappings. As for me, in the hot sunshine I would just wear a short sleeve shirt and skirt, and my exposed skin would often be sunburned. Chuang's multi-layer protected face, hands, and legs had never been exposed to sunlight and were so fair that they were envied by all of us. On the other hand, looking at myself, I was the one to be blamed because I was too lazy to protect my skin. However, I never paid much attention and adopted the attitude whatever will be will be.

Still, seeing someone else's fair skin ... oh yes, I envied it, there was no doubt about it. However, I had no desire to learn from her how to become more diligent about making myself up. No wonder my mother often nagged at me, saying that some of my age-group friends were already married and had kids, while no one even courted me. A classmate of mine got married at the age of 16, and became a grandma before she turned 40. At the time of this writing,[45] she was about 60 and a great-grandmother. I think it all has to do with a person's interests and destiny, which cannot be controlled. Not long ago, this former classmate, who was such a beauty when she was young, came for a visit. She spoke of the then-young lady co-ops, and we all laughed uncontrollably as we recounted some of the funny things that had happened back then. Inevitably, what came up was the subject of her envy-producing fair skin. I asked her whether she still used banana tender leaves to cover up her skin when she worked. She laughed loudly, and lamented: "What banana leaves? I'd forgotten all about it until you mentioned it. After I got married, I had borne seven kids non-stop, in addition to endless work on the farm. See, I have lost almost all of my teeth; how could I care for the skin?" What she said was true. Other than her skin, which was whiter than mine just as it had been before, she did look like a woman close to sixty years of age, one who had been working under the hot sun for a long time. The passage of many years had had no mercy on her; it candidly marked every bit of life and its many hardships upon her once-youthful face.

---

45. The Chinese edition of this book was published in 2003.

4. Episodes From My Early Tsou Life

My Hair Stories

Mother's Only Pair of Scissors

I grew up in a poor family in a remote village. Due to malnutrition, my coarse hair always looked like a bunch of dried straw. I remember when I was in the elementary school, there were rules on hair styles. To comply with the rules, for a period of time, I had to stand in front of my mother to receive her torture. Although Mother called out to me with her tender, loving voice, "Paiz, time to have a haircut," I was afraid to see in Mother's hand her only pair of scissors—the pair that was used for all purposes, be it cutting paper, cutting hair, anything. When she thought the scissors weren't sharp enough, she would whip them a few times on Father's whetstone. They might be sharp enough for cutting certain things, but not enough to cut hair.

Although my hair was dry, it wasn't easy for Mother's all-purpose scissors; the hair often slipped from the scissors. Mother's mouth would synchronize with the scissors: She opened her mouth when the scissor blades were open, closed her mouth tightly when the blades were closing to cut the hair; she even ground her teeth left and right as if her mouth movements would make the job easier.

Though her voice was tender, her hands were not dexterous, due to years of hard labor. Besides not having good tools, she needed to handle me, who was behaving like a squirming maggot—not an easy task at all. When I sensed the scissors touching my skin, I would sway my head to the other side, or withdraw my neck and shoulders. These movements often caused Mother's scissors, which didn't grow eyes, to cut the skin on my forehead, or peel off a piece behind my neck. Worse, my ears could even be scratched by the sharp blades, if she was not careful. At the end of a haircut, not only did the hair looked like it had been bitten by a dog, but there were also wounds here and there. The whole hair-cutting process can be described as a major disaster.

From my first grade to the sixth, Mother had purchased a new pair of scissors only once. With new scissors, and as I grew older the ability to actually sit still and be more patient, the calamities were greatly reduced.

My Hair Turned Grey Overnight

When I was about in my second grade, I got up one morning and was especially troubled by my hair; it remained unruly no matter how I combed it. All the adult family members had left to work in the mountains. My eldest brother kept telling me that it was time to go to school. What should I do?

Back then in the primary schools, students attended a national flag raising ceremony first thing in the morning. Afterwards, they entered the classroom and sang songs about personal hygiene rules, and were closely inspected. For example, was the student carrying a handkerchief? Was their face, the area behind the ears, and their fingernails clean? Were their hair and clothes clean and neat? Normally, there was no problem with the clothes since the inspection was carried out early in the morning. The handkerchiefs were carried pretty much for inspection purposes only, and sometimes were kind of dirty. Fingernails? They were tough to keep clean because I, for one, needed to help pick vegetables and peel sweet potatoes, which could easily stain my fingernails. Besides, I liked to play around a lot. How could I keep my fingernails clean with all of these activities? Hair was the only thing I didn't have problems with because Mother always cut it short, when she cut it, so that she didn't need to cut it very often.

But back to dealing with my unruly hair that morning. Probably because I slept too soon after I had washed my hair the night before, and moved about too much while I slept, my hair wasn't neat at all. While I was busy worrying about passing the school hair inspection, I noticed my mother's belongings on a nearby table. Since I didn't care much about doing make-ups, I never really paid attention to how Mother used those things. I only noticed that some were used on her face, others on her hair. Now, under severe time pressure, I hesitantly dug a chunk of some stuff from a container with my finger and applied it to my hair, without looking in a mirror! In a hurry, I followed my brother on the road to school. He didn't notice what had just happened to me.

Every time on my way to school, I would stop by my second aunt's place to pick up the adopted child she helped care for. When my brother and I arrived, they were still having their breakfast. She looked at me with a weird expression, as though she couldn't believe what she saw. Dragging me outside under the sun to get a clear look at my hair, she exclaimed, "Oh my God, what happened? Your hair turned gray overnight!" At first, I was confused, but then suddenly realized what I had done at home with Mother's stuff. I explained this to her. She sniffed my hair and said, "Why'd you apply facial cream on your hair?

It's for your face!" It was too late to wash my hair, so she used a towel to remove the white cream in my hair as much as she could. With my lumpy hair, I arrived at the school. I certainly didn't pass the hair inspection. The teacher asked me what happened, in front of the other students. This was one of the biggest embarrassments in my entire childhood.

My First Hair Perming

It was about two decades ago, around the time China opened up to the world, that I saw on TV some beauty salons in Shanghai. Liberated from decades of prohibitions, they brought out hair perming devices that had been stored for years in the back room. I had never seen such things. Each setting roller was connected to an electrical wire that was plugged into an electrical outlet. Electricity, I learned, is actually used to perm hair! This reminds me of the Taiwanese expression for perming hair; it's called "electrifying hair." The expression must have originated from the way perming hair was done in the past. Maybe I wasn't born early enough to witness the kind of perming devices that were used then in Shanghai salons. However, because of the rapid economic development in China, businesses of all kinds, including the salon business, for sure, have introduced the most avant-garde technologies from abroad. These days, you see salons everywhere in China, be they on main streets or in small alleys. Hair perming technologies and devices, available in other countries, are also now available in China. They are keeping pace with the outside world.

After I finished attending school, I let my straw-like hair grow long. But I would never look like the beautiful actresses in the movies, the ones you see caressing their soft, smooth hair in front of a mirror.

One day in my late teens, Mother apparently couldn't tolerate my sloppy look any longer.

She said to my father: "Give Paiz some money for her to perm her hair in Hopiana.[46] She already looks like a wild woman, now her unruly hair makes her even more so." Mother always combed her hair neatly, with a bun hairstyle behind her head.

Early one morning I walked for three hours to Hopiana. With a deep breath, I entered the beauty salon, the only one in the town. Actually, this salon had been around for many years; you couldn't miss it when you were on your way to the train station. Although I had been to town often, I had never noticed the salon's existence because I felt it had nothing to do with me.

Inside, there were customers waiting. They were Han women, with fair skin.[47]

In stark comparison, my physical appearance was so different from theirs that I could barely raise my head. The salon owner was the sole beautician. When I saw villagers with long or short, curled hair, I knew that it had been permed, but I had no idea how it was done. I sat in the waiting room, listening to the other customers. One said that she wanted to have her hair washed. Well, I had always washed my own hair, not knowing until now that with money, the task could be done by someone else. This experience really opened up my eyes!

---

46. *The contemporary name is* Fun-Chi Fu *(*奮起湖*).* Hopi *is the Tsou's word for "a water scoop made of a bottle-gourd." The lower land of the town looks like a water scoop made of a bottle-gourd, and therefore is named* Hopiana*; "ana" means a "place."*
47. *Later immigrants to Taiwan are more fair-skinned people, and are labeled as Han (*漢人*).*

I continued sitting there, motionless, watching the owner's every movement. Then, someone told the beautician that she wanted to have her hair permed. This interested me, since I was here for the same reason. I wanted to see how it was done.

First, the beautician asked the customer how long she wanted her hair to be, and then began to swiftly trim her hair. Her scissors really made me envious; I wished my mother had owned a pair of scissors as sharp as hers when she cut my hair! After the beautician finished trimming she divided the hair into small bundles, and inserted each through a central slit of rubber sheet. She then wet each bundle, rolled it up with an iron rod, and tightened it with a rubber band. She dipped a small bag of some kind of chemical briefly in the water, squeezed it a little, then clipped it with a bundle of rolled up hair. Every time she clipped it, you heard a sizzling *"zzzzzz"* sound accompanied by smoke! I was so scared that I wanted to leave the salon! Alas, I stayed because I didn't want to be looked down upon by other customers. Besides, how would I face my mother if I didn't get my hair permed? I just patiently waited for my turn.

I told the beautician to perm my hair short. Sitting in the salon chair, I could see for the first time my entire humble self in front of a big mirror. It was a novel experience, one I never had experienced; at home I used a small mirror on a table. Through the large mirror, I could see the beautician behind me—the most fashionable lady in our remote village. How different we looked! What a contrast!

Frying Fish

It was scary enough to see someone undergoing hair perming,

but it was even more scary when you yourself were the one. The chemical bag had to be squeezed correctly after being dipped in water, otherwise it wouldn't have its intended effect. If the concoction was too dry, boiling liquid could run to the adjacent skin—mine!—and burn it. The beautician (and the boss) kept reminding me to let her know if I felt intense heat somewhere, in which case she could lean over and blow air to the area. She would continue to ask, "Is it still too hot?" until it had cooled down to a tolerable temperature. I was very scared, so much so that before she pinned the bag to a bundle of my hair, before I heard the sizzling "zzzzzz" like what you'd hear when frying fish in a hot pan, I would withdraw my neck and grab tightly the arm rests of the chair. I vaguely remember she did it for about twenty-some curls of hair, and every time I felt like a fish to be fried in a hot pan. Actually, one skin area was burned so badly that blisters developed. Sigh! I never realized one had to suffer so much to have a beautiful hairdo. On the other hand, I couldn't run away when the hair was done halfway.

BBQ

All the curls were finished; the weight of my head seemed to have doubled, making me feel my neck had difficulty supporting it! The boss wrapped my head with a towel and told me to sit in another chair, while she was attending other customers. When the bags were cool enough, she removed the devices on my head in a reverse order of the earlier process. My hair was indeed curled! She then asked me to sit next to a sink and lower my head, so she could wash my hair. She used a water scoop made of a bottle-gourd to scoop room-temperature water from a water tank and mix with some hot water in a bucket. Because this was the first time I ever had my hair permed, I acted like a puppet, following her commands one at a time since I didn't know what might come next.

After my hair was washed, she used hair curlers with spikes to roll up my hair in small bundles. When finished, she had me sit facing a fire stove in order to dry my hair. At that time, there was no electricity in the remote village. Once in a while, more charcoal had to be added to the stove lest the fire die out. When that happened, and it did, the beautician would have to carry the stove to the salon entrance, add some new charcoal, and wave a fan to help the charcoal catch fire. The waving stirred up charcoal dust to all corners of the room and onto the customers. I felt as if I were a piece of meat, baked on the stove and flipped over from time to time. Because a head is round, I needed to change its position in relation to the stove, so that my hair could be dried evenly.

At last, my hair was dried and the beautician unrolled the curlers. Because there was no electricity, there was no hair dryer; my hair was simply combed and sprayed. That ended the torture that had lasted for a few hours. As a result of being constantly tense, I was very exhausted once it was over. Looking at a mirror, I saw someone whom I seemed to know. Beautiful? I thought the money I spent made me look like an ogre. Not used to the way I looked, I wasn't comfortable seeing myself in the mirror.

After leaving the salon, I purchased some groceries at Hopiana as requested by my parents. On the way home, I only wished not to see any acquaintances.

High Mountain Girl Goes to the City

First visit to Chia-yi City

Ah-Mei (阿美) had been to the city when she was a little girl. Even though her parents worked very hard, they didn't have the resources to take her there themselves.[48] However, Ah-Mei was a fortunate girl. She met the very caring teacher, Ma, when she began to attend primary school. Teacher Ma had just been assigned to work at the school of this remote mountain village, and Ah-Mei was in Teacher Ma's class. Every time the teacher saw Ah-Mei—the little girl with big, round eyes—she would stop her, kneel down in front of the young first-grade elementary school pupil, and look at her from side to side while complimenting her beautiful eyes. Actually, Ah-Mei wasn't that different physically from other little girls in the village. What little girl there didn't have big eyes? Her skin color was even darker than that of other girls![49] At first, the innocent Ah-Mei wasn't sure about Teacher Ma's compliments, because no one else, other than her mother, had treated her that well.

Initially, Ah-Mei wasn't comfortable with Teacher Ma's special attention, especially the close-up look at her. Teacher Ma's skin was

---

48. *In this, the book's only piece written in the third person, Ah-Mei is a pseudonym for the author, Paiz Mukunana, which was changed to Faisu Mukunana in 2007.*
49. *The general public's sentiment at the time was in favor of fair skin.*

beautifully fair, tinged with pink. In contrast Ah-Mei's appearance was sloppy, and sometimes her face showed traces of a runny nose, all of which made her feel ashamed and uneasy. Gradually, though, Ah-Mei became used to Teacher Ma, and understood why she admired her big eyes so much. Ah-Mei realized that the teacher's eyelids were puffy, as if after a big cry, and when the teacher looked at her, she looked through a narrow slit between her eyelids.

Ah-Mei's mother knew that Teacher Ma liked her daughter, and often told people that Ah-Mei was fortunate. She would frequently offer Teacher Ma something that was available at home, such as ripe papaya from the top of papaya trees, or vegetables from the garden. Ah-Mei's mother would wrap up the harvests in a sheet of cloth and ask Ah-Mei to bring it to school for her teacher.

One day, Teacher Ma stopped Ah-Mei again, and said to her: "I will go to Chia-yi (嘉義) when the summer recess begins. Would you want to go with me?" At this time, Ah-Mei was already very close with Teacher Ma. Not thinking that she should check with her mother first, all she thought about was what she had heard about the city being an exciting place, with lots of houses and motor vehicles people referred to as "moving houses." She had also heard of something called "electric light bulbs." They were unlike the kerosene lamps she had at home, or before that when they used dried castor seeds from the field strung together with a bamboo stick for burning and creating light. The smoke from both darkened their nostrils when they stayed close to it to do homework. The so-called electric light bulbs could light up a room as if it were day time—so bright that even a jumping lice could be seen! In Chia-yi there were also many high-class stores selling beautiful goods, unlike that dingy, dark, and small store owned by Old

Man Ah-Gie—as if Ah-Gie didn't want his customers to notice that the goods he sold were only suitable for the second- or even lower-classes. Ah-Mei thought she must see such a place as Chia-yi, and accepted Teacher Ma's invitation immediately.

She returned home and told her mother all about it. In response, her mother said, "It's really not a good idea to burden your teacher." Eventually, however, she gave in to her daughter's request. "Oh my, this is not a dream, I will visit Chia-yi!" Ah-Mei cried, wishing that day would quickly arrive.

That day finally did arrive. Unfortunately, a typhoon raged in the area, cutting off railway transportation. They decided to take a mountain trail, hiking on foot for nearly seven hours to Tsu-Ko (觸□), and then ride a bus to Chia-yi. As a matter of fact, it took about the same amount of time between this route and another route—Hopiana on foot followed by a train from Hopiana to Chia-yi. It would only take two hours to Hopiana! But little Ah-Mei was so excited that she couldn't wait; besides, walking long-distance didn't bother her because everyone in the village was so used to walking no matter where they were going, including Chia-yi. However, because she was so excited to be going to the city, she wished she could fly there instantly, and feel no fatigue at all when she arrived.

En route, Teacher Ma shared the lunch she'd prepared at home, called kitten's ears. It was made of slightly salty, thin dough that in turn was made of flour and shaped like a cat's ears. Ah-Mei had never had it before, and she liked it.

At last, they arrived at Tsu-Ko and took a bus for Chia-yi. Ah-Mei was so exhilarated. She finally was on a vehicle that she always heard people call "moving house." She looked out the bus windows and tried not to blink her big eyes, lest she would miss something. Alas, Ah-Mei was tired after the long trip on foot; she fell asleep. Nearing their destination, Teacher Ma woke her up: "Wake up! We are arriving in Chia-yi soon." Opening her eyes, she saw house after house; some were really tall. All things were novel to her.

She wondered: How do people climb up and walk down in these houses? Initially, she thought the inhabitants might have to use a long bamboo ladder, as her family did in order to reach the attic, which was used as a millet storage space. People here, she reasoned, would have to have a really long bamboo ladder for these tall houses!

It was early evening when they arrived at Chia-yi. Teacher Ma took Ah-Mei to a house called "hotel."

"Ah, that thing called light bulb, it's really bright!" she exclaimed, "and there are stairs!" She stared with big eyes at that thing called stairs, and really wanted to step on them to get a feel. "Would it sway as the bamboo ladder does at home?" she murmured. Ah-Mei restrained herself from running around, remembering Mother's words to do only what Teacher Ma allowed her to do. After Teacher Ma finished checking-in at the hotel reception, she turned around and took Ah-Mei to the stairs that headed to the rooms above. This was the first time Ah-Mei ever walked on indoor stairs, and noticed they didn't sway! She was so excited that she felt like running up and down the stairs and screaming loudly at the same time.

Once in the room, Teacher Ma told Ah-Mei to take a bath, before going out for dinner. After eating, they strolled the streets, which were gradually lit by the street lights. The teacher took Ah-Mei to the famous Central Fountain, where Ah-Mei was stunned to see water going up instead of flowing down, as it would normally do. Sometimes it spewed up high; other times, much lower. Under the night lighting, this fountain looked even more fascinating. Neither Ah-Mei's eyes or feet could move away from the beautiful scene.

The stores in Chia-yi were all lit up with electric light bulbs, and inside the stores there were countless beautiful things. Ah-Mei was amazed, her eyes more wide-open than ever. After the dinner, the loving, caring Teacher Ma bought her a pair of shoes, covering up her slender, dark-skin feet. Ah-Mei was so used to barefoot walking, the new shoes made it difficult for her to walk, and she would have stumbled if Teacher Ma hadn't held her hands. They immediately became a burden to her, but Ah-Mei wasn't courageous enough to let Teacher Ma know that she wanted to remove them.

There were so many novelties on the street that attracted her attention; later that night her eyes became tired and dried out.

Teacher Ma also bought her many things not available in her mountain village, such as an ice pop. This was something you could only let melt in your mouth. If swallowed it would hurt your throat as hot food would. Teacher Ma also bought something called "chewing gum." Ah-Mei studied the picture on the wrapping paper that showed a princess blowing a bubble with bubblegum, and learned to do the same. What a wonderful thing that could be played with and tasted at the same time! When she went to bed, she kept the gum in her mouth. It was still there the next morning when she awoke.

The Grown-up Ah-Mei

Many years had passed, and Ah-Mei was now a grown-up lady. She and her friend Ah-Siang went together to visit the city. Ah-Siang had been to Chia-yi often. The city had more things going on than the last time Ah-Mei had visited. The place she wanted to visit most was that miraculous Central Fountain, because it was at the center of the city, and because there were many movie theaters around it. Villagers would always watch a few movies when they visited, to make the arduous trip worthwhile, and Ah-Mei was no exception. She couldn't figure out why the actors and actresses were all so beautiful. When she watched a movie of tragedy, following the story plot, she would cry hard and be sad. When the movie ended she would feel empty-hearted, because her heart had been hijacked by the movie stars! It was a feeling of not knowing how to carry on her own life from that point on.

As a grown-up, she wanted to learn how to make herself look nice, just like others did. Shy as she was, Ah-Mei hurried into a store with her friend. She quickly purchased lip sticks and facial cream, and left just as fast, as though they'd done something wrong. Having purchased lip sticks, they reasoned there was no need to purchase cheek colors, because they had seen the senior women in the village apply a small amount of lip stick to their palms, smooth it out with both hands rubbing each other, and then color their cheeks. Ah-Mei also purchased a pair of inch-high high heel shoes.

On the second day, she felt exhausted due to all the shopping; her feet were sore and her legs ached. It was very strange that she never felt tired working in the mountains. "Why does walking on the leveled streets makes me exhausted?" she wondered. Later that day, she found out the reason. Her friend Ah-Siang asked her why she raised her heels so high. Ah, the reason was that Ah-Mei wasn't used to walking on level ground; she was used to walking on mountain trails! There, she always raised her heels high, and then stepped down vigorously lest she be tripped by something and fall. No wonder she was tired! Years later, whenever she recalled how ugly-looking she must have appeared because of the way she walked, she still scolded herself for being a country bumpkin.

One time, Ah-Mei and her friend Ah-Siang were taking a bus to somewhere or other. There were many people waiting. They let others board first. When it was their turn, they stood by the bus door. While the bus was moving, Ah-Mei noticed the bus driver looking at her from time to time. This made her nervous. Why was he watching her? "Does he see me as a country bumpkin, does he see me as a beautiful …? " A-Mei was lost in thought, thinking that perhaps the driver was fond of her. Later on, after riding buses for many years, she knew the bus driver was not looking specifically at her, but simply in his rear view mirror to make sure that the passengers were all OK, for safety reasons. She felt ashamed and blushed when thinking of this earlier episode.

Dried Mesona Grass

Many years ago, when summer arrived we would hear the street vendors shouting: "Dried mesona grass!" Sometimes older ladies in the neighborhood would stop a vendor and surround him, eyeing the dried and shiny mesona grass loaded behind his bicycle seat. They would then inspect and touch the dried grass, and begin negotiating for a price. Once in a while, someone might purchase a bundle of it and take it home to slow cook it, and then use the liquid to make light and cold deserts for family members. In later years, these vendors disappeared, and "Dried mesona grass!" wasn't heard anymore. The mesona vendors were replaced by owners of ice drink shops, calling out "Dried mesona grass jelly ice!" to solicit customers.

Nowadays, the more successful ice drink shops don't need to call out anything to get business, and even serve warm mesona grass jelly in the winter time! Once only available in summer as a cool dessert, after just a few years it has also become a popular warm food item for the winter months—thanks to business people's quick thinking. Normally, when I saw a new food product, if the price was reasonable I would try it out. The warm mesona grass jelly was no exception. After the first taste, I thought it was all right, except it lacked the genuine flavor of true mesona grass. I suspect another kind of jelly was used instead. This reminds me of *awkeo* (愛玉) jelly sold in the market that doesn't use the genuine *awkeo* ingredient. One reason is that there isn't that much *awkeo* available, so other ingredients are added.[50]

Mesona grass, nicknamed Cool Jelly Grass (涼粉草), is an annual grass. It germinates in the spring, grows to a height of tens of centimeters. Its stem is square with a bifurcated, minute, hair-like structure on its surface. Its leaves are oval-shaped, with saw-tooth edges, and the backs of the leaves are covered with a hair-like structure as well. It thrives in the sunny areas of the mountainsides, blossoms in the fall, and when the seeds are mature they drop onto the ground and germinate the next spring. There are two varieties of mesona grass: One has red stems and leaf veins, while in the other both the stems and leaves are green. After mesona grass is sun dried you slow-cook it, filter out the leaves and stems, and then add starch to the juice. When it has cooled down it becomes a jelly-like substance. Sugar water is added prior to consumption.

Along with the fond memory of the mesona-picking season when I was a child, and the warm jelly I ate that warmed my heart, a memorable event that had been buried in my mind for several decades suddenly popped up. It was a time of hardship, a time of struggling to survive. I recall that the last name of the principal of our primary school was Lin; his first name completely skips my mind. As a stu-

Freshly harvested *awkeo* fruits before being skinned. *Awkeo* is native to Taiwan.

50. Awkeo, *a member of the fig family, is found only in Taiwan. Its seeds, when in contact with water, produce a jelly-like substance which is the main ingredient for* awkeo *ice jelly.*

dent of junior grade, I remembered him as being lean, tall, and with fair skin; his voice was clear, and his manners affable. The first rice tamale that I ever had—it was wrapped in bamboo leaves—was made by his wife, assisted by several mothers of the students who helped to wrap and cook them. They prepared these rice tamales for close to one hundred students. Naturally, they were not as well made as they are today; back then they were prepared with only chives and salt. But in those impoverished times, they tasted delicious, as if they were out of this world.

Principal Lin was truly an educator. He always put the students first. Alas, he left when I was in my third grade. Our principal was sympathetic with the majority of the students who had no choice but to wear old and torn clothes all year around, because he understood the financial difficulties their parents faced. So he came up with an idea to ease the situation. Noticing that some villagers picked mesona grass, had it dried, and then sold at the market led him to think of a way to make money. He assembled his students in groups, with each consisting of students across different grades, and then assigned a senior to be the group leader. During the regularly scheduled weekly "environment maintenance hour" each group leader took his students to pick mesona grass in the mountains.

The maintenance hour was originally designed for the students to keep the school yard clean and in good order, and to learn about agriculture by planting various kinds of vegetables in the school's backyard. You might ask, "Why did we students plant vegetables?" It was an opportunity for those whose families had farm land to learn about how to spread seeds, weed, and even to fertilize vegetables by using human waste from school's septic tanks. In addition, the students maintained a garden for the teachers who used to live in the cities. Here in the high mountains, there was no market, and stores were far away. Sometimes we used the hour to pick dried twigs for the teachers' cooking use, because there was no electricity or natural gas for cooking or boiling water. If we didn't perform these tasks the teachers would not know how to live their daily lives, as they had never done this type of manual work before. In our impoverished environment, what we did for the teachers was necessary in order to keep them coming to our school! Of course, when students took time out to pick mesona grass, they continued with these chores.

Following our group leader, we went to a mountain chosen by the group. Whether male or female, once released from the classrooms we were like a bunch of monkeys, excited and happy; we roamed in the wild, full of laughter and happy screams that could be heard far away. Barehanded and without any hand tools, we pulled up mesona grass from among the wild grasses, yanking the grass with our right hand and then placing it under the left armpit. A luckier group—it does take luck to actually find the grass!— could quickly collect a lot of it, which they then tied into bundles with rattan vine. Each group member would carry a bundle back to school; stronger students carried heavier bundles. Because we were not allowed to carry knives to school, we used a Stone Age technology to gather the rattan vine. We put the rattan on a rock and hand-held a piece of stone to hammer the rattan repeatedly until it was cut off.

Our principal required us to return from the grass hunting before the school's closing hour, so that students could go home on time. That was because he was aware that their parents had work for them: husking rice, gathering firewood, taking a water buffalo to a grassland, or caring for their younger siblings. Therefore, it was important that the students not arrive home late, keeping in mind that it would take some of them more than an hour's walk to get there. Sometimes, by a stroke of luck, we could quickly pick enough mesona grass in less than the expected amount of time. When that happened, rather than heading straight back to school we spent the leftover time enjoying ourselves by climbing trees and swinging on branches, or hunting edible wild fruits or grass stems in the grasslands. We knew that there were always edible wild fruits there, regardless of the season. With all the roaming and working in the wild we did, we kids had appetites as big as a buffalo's; our stomachs could be filled anytime with anything.

When we'd had enough fun and it was time to go, the group leader led us back to school. Back then, no one wore a watch. We relied on our ability to tell time by judging the position of the sun. We could tell by the sun's location as seen from a mountain top, from a valley, or between one side of a mountain to the other. Experience was everything!

The next morning, we spread the mesona grass on the slopes of the school yard for sun drying, and then placed them on the classroom corridor before school was over.[51] If we had good weather, it would take three or four days for the grass to completely dry; if it wasn't fully dry mildew could grow upon it. After countless picking trips, the mountains had been well covered by the students, and the dried mesona grass was piled up like a mountain itself upon the school walkway.

---

51. *In Taiwan, outside a row of classrooms there is a covered, connected walkway to allow students and teachers to walk from classroom to classroom when it rains. The walkway can also be used for activities in inclement weather.*

Of course, none of the mountain land owners complained about our excursions. They were thankful for the principal's idea to gather the grass in order to help the village children, some of whom were probably theirs.

As a young child fooling around all of the time, I didn't notice when the mountain of dried mesona grass at school was removed. One day, the principal brought with him a stranger to take measurements of each student in order to make them uniforms. When I heard the word "uniform," I didn't understand what it meant and was told by an older student that each one of us would be wearing the same kind of clothes. A long time afterwards, villagers carried bag after bag of unknown materials, revealed later as these uniforms. We kids jumped around excitedly when the principal distributed them to us when school was over. That night, I embraced the uniform as I slept, with my mind filled with satisfaction and happiness. I might have even laughed out loud!

We are all thankful and indebted to our principal for his love, care, and thoughtfulness—for enabling us to receive what we needed through our own efforts, and for delighting our parents as well.

Aboriginal Kids' Snacks

How Sweet the Sugar Balls!

As I remember, the first time I ever spent money to buy candies was when I was already attending the primary school. The only candies at that time were hard sugar balls dusted with sugar granules, called *kama* in the Taiwanese language.

Because transportation systems weren't yet established when I was a child, our village was remote and isolated. There was not even a single store! We'd heard of things like biscuits, beautifully wrapped candies, toys, and so forth by name only, from the adults' descriptions of the outside world where these delights were to be found, or when the elders were telling stories. Because our family grew some sugar canes near our rice fields or on our dry farmland, when told that the taste of candies was like that of sugar canes we could imagine without much difficulty that candies were sweet.

Back then, it wasn't easy to obtain sugar balls when we wanted them. It took luck. For example, an adult might be going to a place where there was a store; that adult might have some money left over after purchasing family essentials like salt and matches; and that adult might be willing to spend a little to buy some sugar balls for his or her kids, so that they could lick the sugar balls to have a taste of its honey-like sweetness. To enjoy the sugar balls, we didn't have to chew and chew like we did with the sugar canes in order to suck some sweet juice out of them, we just used our tongues.

It may sound unhygienic, but we kids in the remote mountains knew very well how to share things, not only with our siblings, but also with classmates and companions. If there were enough sugar balls for everyone, then each would get a whole sugar ball and we'd all be happy. But what if there were more kids than available sugar balls? Well, one of the kids would break up a sugar ball with their teeth while the other kids would wait, with saliva running in their mouths, for the pieces to be distributed. Of course, some pieces were larger than others, but we wouldn't care as long as each of us got one. If there were only two or three friends to share a sugar ball, to show that we were truly good friends one of us held the sugar ball and each of us took turns licking the ball until it was too small to lick further. Then we'd take turns having the ball in our mouth. When good friends shared a sweet sugar ball at the same time, they murmured their secrets to each other. That feeling of love, of sweetness, and of gratification can't be understood by the kids of the contemporary material-abundant era.

Snacks in the Wild

Although things like candies and cookies were not available to the indigenous kids, it wasn't true that there were no snacks at all. In the vast mountainous regions, the Creator prepared various kinds of snacks for us according to different seasons of the year. Families grew fruit trees in the vicinity of their rice fields and dried farmland, such as peach, plum, guava, orange, citrange, papaya, banana, and sugar canes. In addition, there were wildly grown mulberries, passion fruits, strawberries, raspberries, and paper mulberries. Furthermore, there were wild figs, found only in Taiwan, that had a milk taste, and the bitter tasting, bright red horny-toothed ardisia—known also as Christmas berry and Australian holly—fruits. We competed with flying squirrels for golden-colored wild persimmons, whose juice left your mouths with an astringent taste. The squirrels got them at night, we got them during the day. Even the white-fruit meat inside the ripe, sticky nightshades tasted delicious to us.[52]

Almost all of the fruits tasted either sweet, sour, or astringent, with one exception: the roxbourgh sumac. These fruits are formed in strings and fully ripe in autumn. On the outer sphere of the strings, there is a thin layer of powder, with a taste of salt. On our way to school and on our way home back from school the groups of kids, older and younger, from the 5th and the 6th village districts would watch the older kids climb the sumac trees and wait for them to come down with bundles of the fruit; each one of us would be given a small string of it, and we would lick salt powder from it while we were proceeding.

In the 1940s, an era of material shortage, salt was precious, a reality compounded by the fact that our villages were far away from the ocean. Due to the lack of iodine that is contained in sea salt, when I was a child many of the villagers suffered from thyroid goiter; some of them had large tumors hanging under their throats. Through the eyes of we kids, that was an ugly look. Therefore, we wanted to avoid getting the disease, and did so by licking the fruits of roxbourgh sumac every year when the fruits became ripe. Later on, when transportation

---

52. *The citrange is a citrus hybrid of the sweet orange and the trifoliate orange. The purpose of this cross was to attempt to create a cold hardy citrus tree.*

improved and it became easier to obtain salt, thyroid goiter disease was gradually eradicated.

Not only did we enjoy tree fruits, there were many underground growths that could serve as snacks. One example is the stem of kudzu vines, which could relieve thirst when chewed and, according to village folklore, be good for the stomach and spleen. In the spring, on the sloped meadow adjacent to the school, the underground stems were white and full. Someone, a daredevil who must have tried all kinds of grasses, discovered that these white stems were edible. As the daredevil's disciples, we kids followed him during the noon breaks, and furiously dug up the stems with a bamboo blade. Their taste was rather clear and sweet!

In the late spring and early summer, amid silver grass bushes, once in a while you'd find a silver grass that hadn't grown normally, due to insect bites received during its growing process. As a result, it grew something like the wild rice stem. The abnormal growth could be eaten raw or roasted.

The defectively-grown white fruits on camellia trees, from which is derived Camellia seed oil, also known as tea oil, tasted unforgettably sweet, clear, and cool. However, they were hard to find, because they were the ones that were infested by worms and, as a result, couldn't develop unto normal fruits. Besides, they could only be picked before sunrise, otherwise the color of the fruits would change and the fruits would become inedible.

Maple trees could sometimes develop abnormal fruits too; their juicy taste was a little like that of wax apples. The tender skin of the wild roses tasted a bit sour and could make people salivate in order to quench their thirst. The leaves, fruits, and stems of creeping smartweeds were also edible.

Once in a while, we acted as honey bees to gather flower pollen; be it banana flowers, canna, fuchsia, hibiscus, bluebells, passion flowers, they couldn't escape from our devil hands. However, the honey bees were civilized pollen gatherers, and spread pollen from flower to flower while we were acting as flower destroyers. Fortunately, we were not frequent offenders.

Our Natural Brand of Chewing Gum

When the beginning of an autumn arrives, it reminds me of the parasitic shrubs that grow on branches of other trees. We called them *kupiya*. It also brings back childhood memories that are of unlimited happiness.

Well ahead of autumn's arrival, the village kids began eagerly, "with big open eyes," to look among tree branches for bird-nest-shaped green growth. If they were lucky to find one, they would remember where it was. When autumn came the fruits, which were a little bigger than green beans, would ripen. The kids would climb the tree to reach the fruits, finding a good spot among the branches where they could either stand or sit comfortably. Slowly, they'd pick the ripe fruits that had turned a little yellow, raise their heads slightly, open their mouths, and squeeze the individual fruit from one end until its green fruit meat dropped into their mouths. It tasted sweet and fragrant. What's more, it was sticky!

We'd sit on the branches, relaxed, and squeeze the fruits one by one into our mouths, non-stop. When we had sucked up their sweetness and our mouths were full, the juice became sticky and could be blown as chewing gum would. During the school lunch break, my classmates and I would go to the neighboring camellia tea oil farm to pick *kupiya*. It was so much fun that each one of us would occupy a spot on a tree, stick our tongue out to compare the size of *kupiya* in our mouths, and compete to see who could blow the biggest bubbles. Oftentimes, we enjoyed it so much that we forgot to return to school for afternoon classes, and we would be ordered to stand facing the wall as punishment. For the fun we had, we didn't regret the punishment.

Some naughty male students would stick *kupiya* on other students' heads. That sticky thing, like today's chewing gum, was very difficult to get rid of even with a knife, once it stuck on something. That poor kid with *kupiya* on his head, once back home, would be chased by the angry parents with a stick or bamboo strip, to strike their child for goofing around at the school, for not studying hard, for not cherishing parents' hard work, for only making troubles, and so forth. Whether they could catch him or not was another matter, because normally kids ran faster than their parents could!

The only way to get rid of *kupiya* from the hair was to cut or shave the chunk of hair along with the *kupiya*, which would make the head look like it was infested by some kind of skin disease—a terribly mangy look! During the *kupiya* season, anyone with that kind of ugly haircut, needless to say, would make it obvious to the beholders the story behind it.

Kupiya is exclusively parasitic on other trees, such as mulberries,

Camellias, or maples. *Kupiya* is more like a grass than a shrub; the entire plant is some three to four feet tall. Since it absorbs nutrients from the host tree, it often causes the host branches to decay and rot. According to our folk medicine, its leaves and stems can be used as herbal medicines and its fruits are good for eyes.

There were abundant wild grasses and wild fruits in the mountains, where my friends and I lived during a time when the entire area was not developed. This enabled us to spend our happy childhoods in a natural environment. Perhaps kids back then were especially adventurous, with mouths so indiscriminate that everything to them was edible and tasty. True or not, our rambling in the wild, our searching for snacks and having much fun while we were at it, not only satisfied our taste buds' desires, but also gave us a sense of accomplishment. These activities provided us kids with opportunities to learn about the basic survival skills in the wild, and have many marvelous adventures and experiences.

Wood Clogs[53]

Upon reaching a certain age, a person tends to become nostalgic. As the saying goes, "Young people live in their dreams, middle-age people live in reality, and the older people live in their nostalgia." It's very true. I have noticed many older people who might forget where they put things a short moment ago but vividly remember details of their childhood. I have seen an elder, nearly 90 years of age, behave like a child of seven or eight, saying things like "My mother was such a so and so," relating something about his mother and acting like a spoiled brat—while actually yearning for her love in return. Even though the elder I am recalling was full of gray hair, his facial expressions were so childishly lovely.

Oh my! Why do I always recall my early childhood? Is it because I am that old? I'm not really that old. I think it's just because I like to revisit past events to which I can never return, nor they to me.

I am here at the historic street of Hsin-Chuang (新莊) to purchase supplies for the Lunar New Year, leisurely strolling and looking around at the mountainous selections in each store. Whether for meals, for practical use and daily chores (items like soap, towels, brooms, pots, etc.), or for clothing they have everything you could possibly need.

---

53. *Author's note: This article was awarded Master Piece in 1999 at the First Annual Essay Competition of the Aboriginal Literature sponsored by Chung-Hwa Automobile Co.*

Suddenly, I hear the familiar sound of clogs, though yet quite far away. I turn around to look for the source and notice a young lady wearing a pair of wood clogs; this is something I haven't seen, or heard, for a long, long time, and it makes me nostalgic. As she approaches I can tell that the wood clogs she wears are expensive and well made; they are most likely imported from Japan.

Strolling at this historic street in the early afternoon, before evening market opens, there is a big contrast between the quietness now and the noisy atmosphere that will commence come evening. At this quiet time, hearing the "*ko, ko, ko*" from wood clogs gives me somewhat unsettled feelings. I worry whether the sound might wake up the old store owner who sits in a broken chair dozing off. I worry whether the sound might remind him, as it does me, of the times when most people wore wood clogs that knocked the ground and made the "*ko, ko, ko*" sound everywhere.

It is not that I enjoyed wearing wood clogs so much that it made me recall the era when everyone wore them. As a matter of fact, I disliked wearing them, especially the ones that used straps going through the space between the big toe and the second toe. Unfortunately (of all things!), those were the kind of wood clogs my *amo* (father) liked to have for the family members. When I was small, I preferred bare feet to wearing those kind of clogs, even after a bath when I had just washed my feet and before I hopped into my bed—times when I wanted my feet clean of dirt from the dirt floor! The discomfort from wearing them might have stemmed from the fact that my tiny, slender toes could not tolerate very well the stress caused by the straps. Unfortunately, during the times when there was a shortage of material goods, life, as my husband used to tell me, could be summed up like this: "Poor people eat what food they have and use what things they have. But the rich can have whatever they want." And because of that, for me and my family there was no choice: We took the free clogs! Today, however, what strikes my mind has nothing to do with wearing wood clogs, but, rather, the memory of how they were made.

When I was around eight years old, living in the remote Alishan mountain region where our house stood out by itself, it was rare to have any visitors. Once in a while, though, depending upon the season of the year, one would arrive to either procure dried bamboo shoots or palm tree sheaths. One day, when my younger brother and I were playing in the yard, suddenly we noticed a group of people with shoulder poles, walking down the mountain trail in the back of our bamboo house.

"They are not Tsou people," Brother proclaimed. He knew this because our people would carry a basket, not shoulder poles, made of rattan and placed on their heads to carry things; carrying a basket on the head was good for walking on a narrow, winding mountain trail. My brother and I were always very scared when we saw them, because it was quite rare to see strangers, especially the Han people. I quickly picked up my younger sister and ran as fast as possible with my brother toward our bamboo house, while crying out "*putu, putu,* there are *putus!*"[54] Upon hearing our cries our *amo* emerged from the house and greeted them as they arrived at our dirt yard. We kids hid behind the doors and the windows, showing only our heads so that we could peek and watch to see what these *putus* were after.

---

54. Putu *means Han people.*

It was only a few years after the end of the World War II, and there was no common language that people could use to communicate with each other, therefore the Tsou language was used among the Tsou people and Japanese was used among other tribes. My *amo* and one of the *putus* babbled *"i-li-wa-la"* in Japanese for quite some time, while the rest of the *putus* were chatting among themselves. Amo then came into the house and told us that these *putus* wanted to make wood clogs. We, full of naiveté, asked, "What wood clogs? They come *here* to make clogs?" We knew what wood clogs were but didn't know exactly what material wood clogs were made of.

My *ino* (mother) said: *"Putu* trees are cut down to make wood clogs. (We called tung oil trees *putu* trees—i.e., Han people trees—probably because the trees were introduced to us by the Han people.) Since the location of the trees to be removed would elicit great concerns in my heart, I asked Mom desperately: "Where will the *putu* trees be cut down?" The area above the Japanese road was her answer.

The Japanese roads were built by the Japanese authoritative government, which ruled Taiwan between 1895 and 1945, in order to conveniently control the various Tsou tribes. The government ordered the Tsou people to not only build the roads, but to travel on them as well. The roads were later broadened and improved to allow use by jeeps. When the Japanese left Taiwan in 1945, the Tsou abandoned these broad and winding roads, preferring to take their old shortcut trails; this was because the Tsou were accustomed to thick woods and steep rocky paths in the high mountains where they could climb and race like goats and deer. This was more in keeping with their free-spirited way of doing things. A nature-loving people, the Tsou didn't like rigidly conceived and executed infrastructure like the roads the Japanese built, preferring to roam in the wild taking small trails or no trails at all. After the Japanese surrendered in 1945, they were free to do as they pleased, and they did.

Upon hearing that the *putu* trees—those on the land above the road built during the Japanese period of governance—would be cut down, it felt like my heart was being cut down as well. You know, between late spring and early summer the *putu* trees' white flowers fully blossom, causing the mountains to turn white. This was such a beautiful scene! When you stood on the right ridge of the mountains with the breeze coming along the Tseng-wen River (曾文溪) and blowing to the mountains (southern winds in the early summer), they looked like white ocean waves, wave after wave after wave—how beautiful to see! (At the time, I had never seen an ocean. This was based on my younger uncle's description of the oceans that he had seen.)

After the arrival of October, whenever we had time, we adults and kids carried woven bags with us when we went to the *putu* tree woods. By that time of year, the leaves had all fallen to the ground. We cleared away with our hands the fallen leaves and searched for treasures—the treasures of ripe fruits fallen from the *putu* trees! Although the shape of the fruit is round, and about the same size as the native guava, its surface area is not all smooth but covered with what look like uneven, bumpy veins. On beautiful, sunny autumn days the fruits could be so ripe that they'd drop to the ground and the impact could cause them to break up, and the nuts inside (about five of them, the size of chestnuts) would be scattered all over the sloping hills. Whenever we saw dried skin of the fruits somewhere on the ground, we knew the nuts couldn't be too far away. We carried the fruits home and piled them up. Whenever any family member had spare time, they would use anything, such as nails or metal spoons, to pry nuts off the shells. They'd sun-dry them, and carry them on their backs to the village shops to exchange for daily commodities.

Year after year, the *putu* trees were strongly associated with our lives and work. We so appreciated their white flowers in the early summer and looked forward to picking their nuts in the late fall. I also heard that some kind of oil could be extracted from *putu* tree nuts for use as an additive to increase the engine power of airplanes, automobiles, and other machines. Although my knowledge is limited, I believe the oil was sometimes also used to make paints.

When I was in my teens, without knowing that the local shops wouldn't buy the villagers' nuts anymore due to the lack of demand from the outside merchants, I watched the villagers pile up tons of *putu* tree nuts around their houses. Later on, I heard that imported petroleum had replaced *putu* nut oil because petroleum performed much better as a fuel.

Of course, I couldn't really complain or express my sadness over the *putu* trees being cut down. I mean, what could I do after Father had made the agreement?! Although there were *putu* woods elsewhere, the merchants must have had good reason to choose this area. It was probably because it was closer to them and full of trees concentrated around one mountain. As a small child, I wouldn't have any leverage to affect adults' decision making anyway, but that didn't stop me from continuing to pop my head by the doors and watch what those *putus* were up to.

After an agreement between Amo and their representative had

been reached, some of those *putus* began to use saws and machetes to cut into what we called the sweet bamboo[55] forest and the Makino Bamboo forest. Because there were many different kinds of bamboo plants available surrounding our bamboo-built house, it took no time at all for each one to carry on their shoulders a bunch of cut bamboos and build a simple shelter for themselves at a corner of our dirt yard. They also used bamboo to make a sleeping platform, construct a simple table, and they gathered stones to build two cooking ovens. They then unloaded their belongings from large bamboo containers— comforters, tools, cooking utensils, food—and placed them where they belonged, while we kids acted like motionless nailed-in objects, watching their every movement.

We saw Amo go out to talk with the *putus*, and then the *putus* went to Amo and talked to him, and later Amo went back again to the *putus* and told them this and that. Meanwhile, my *ino* worked on the house chores as needed. Occasionally she asked me for assistance. When not needed, I went back to stand by the side of the doors to keep an eye on these *putus*. As evening was approaching, several of them returned with dried wood debris from the forest and began making a fire to cook dinner. When the cooking was finished, they placed a piece of pork on the table, among other things (due to the distance, I could not see the details very well), and began to light incense sticks to worship their gods.

Through my *amo*, I learned about how the *putus* worshiped their gods, which was very different from the way we Tsou people did. Suddenly, a very loud explosion deafened my ears, louder than

---

55. *Sweet bamboo is also called* Dendrocalamus.

anything I had ever experienced as a kid. My younger brothers and sisters were scared—I could see it in their eyes—so scared that they couldn't even cry. Quickly, I picked up my eldest younger sister and led the eldest younger brother towards my mother; I was so scared I almost fell down. My mother said: "Don't be afraid, that is called *baguchigu*. This is the custom of how *putus* worship their gods." (In our language, we didn't have a word for firecrackers. We used the Japanese expression *baguchigu*.) Shortly after, the person who had frequently spoken with Father entered our house with a piece of pork and some candies; this was his way of thanking us for the convenience we afforded them. Seeing the candies relieved me and my siblings of the scares caused by the firecrackers.

Next day, those *putus* got up very early, each of them carrying hand tools and walking in the direction of the "*putus* woods" above the Japanese Road. Shortly afterwards, we could hear the sounds from felled trees that synchronized with the loud conversation going on among them. Each and every time I heard the sound of a felled tung oil tree—the tree that blossomed such beautiful flowers—my heart felt like it had been knifed, and was full of pain.

The *putus* carried lunch boxes to work, and wouldn't return to their shelter until it started to get dark. Once there, each placed the wood clogs they had made that day upon the ground in the yard to let them dry.

There were two types of clogs. One, as mentioned before, had a strap that ran between the great toe and the second toe; the clog itself was about one inch thick with the central area under the arch sawed off so that the clog had two roughly one-inch lateral supports underneath—one in the front and one under the heel. This design helped reduce the clog's weight and at the same time keep the wearer's feet above the ground. The shape of a clog was somewhat rectangular, roughly resembling the shape of a human foot. The second type of clogs they made looked like modern day slippers, i.e., with a belt nailed from side to side across the frontal section of the foot across the toes. The first type was worn by men, the second by women.

As I said, these *putus* went to work in early morning and returned to rest after sunset. When the pile of wood clogs on the yard grew large enough, they would carry them, using a pole across their shoulders, to the train station in Hopiana, and let the train transport the clogs to the cities. At that time, trains were the sole means of transportation. It would take at least two and a half hours to carry goods on foot from our house in the valley to Hopiana, and that was by someone who was used to working in and walking through the demanding terrain. There was no doubt that these workers worked extremely hard! Alas, I had little sympathy for them, because they stole away from my heart those beautiful "white waves" of the tung oil trees. Picture in your mind, as I am now, how when the winds blew across the mountain, the white leaves of these magnificent trees were like the wind-driven spray of waves upon the ocean.

When the *putu* trees were all felled, it was time for the *putus* to go home. I have no knowledge of the number of pairs of wood clogs they had made; all I knew was that all of the *putu* trees were gone and all of the white *putu* tree waves were also gone—forever. I couldn't help feeling something was amiss in my little heart.

In my memory, the *putus* who came to our village in the early fall and stayed for about two months were the ones who made wood clogs. But not long after that, another group of *putus* came who wanted to harvest bamboos because it was the best time of year for this.

"Why do they harvest bamboos?" we asked Amo. This time, we siblings were not as curious about the *putus* as we were last time, when we saw them every day. Amo replied: "Bamboos can be used to make wood clogs." "Bamboos can be used to make wood clogs?" asked our eldest brother, who was away from home at school when the *putus* were here to harvest the tung oil trees. Replied Amo: "Bamboos are to be sliced and flattened and then, to be glued onto the clogs, so that color drawings can be done on it to make clogs very beautiful." Who cares? Every day I was bare-footed to go to school, to work in the mountains. Beautiful clogs had nothing to do with my life! I was still unhappy because of the loss of the white *putu* tree waves. Amo continued anyway, adding: "Those clogs are suitable only for city-dweller wearing."

Of course, we couldn't care less about wearing any of the several dozen pairs of the wood clogs given to Amo by the boss of the clog makers before he left. These were not-quite-finished clogs. With his fine skills, Amo used a red-hot iron spike to burn three holes through the clogs, and passed through them hand-made string of cloth or palm fibers. He then tied a knot under the clogs, and they were ready to be worn.

My *amo* was a great man. He was a hardworking man of responsibility and integrity who showed great respect to the elders. He was a great father much respected by us all. The only thing I wasn't happy with him about was that he didn't seem to treat boys and girls differently. He wanted me, as a girl, to wear this type of wood clogs?! But what could you do? Before the clog-maker boss left, he asked Amo what type of clogs he wanted. Alas, he chose the ones I have just described.

After the Makino Bamboo forest was clear cut, it revealed barren steep slopes and looked like the *putu* tree forest after it was clear cut. "But," said Amo, "Makino Bamboo forest will grow back. The land that used to be *putu* tree forest will be cleared by the end of the year to grow millet and sweet yam, alternating with *putu* trees. They grow really fast; in six, seven years they will bloom and bear nuts again." To support the family's livelihood, our hardworking *amo* had his plan, for sure. Delighted, I thought I would be able to see my beloved white waves in six or seven years! As long as there was no worry over eating and playing, an innocent little child could always fill her heart with hope.

It wasn't until the following year that I learned that Amo sold *putu* trees and Makino Bamboos to raise funds for building our new house. Otherwise, where would money come from to do it?

Due to the flourishing plastic industry and its ceaseless production of plastic products, abundant styles of beautiful plastic slippers filled the market—and wood clogs were gradually forgotten. Once in a while, when I see them, I can't help but reminisce about my formative years in the valley, and those endless white waves.

Ak'i's Cleaning Products

For countless generations, the aboriginal people lived in the mountain forests, which provided for their daily needs. However, when the Japanese rulers arrived in Taiwan they encouraged the aborigines to abandon their traditional way of life for one the Japanese considered better and more modern, by using the very latest products. Then, beginning in 1945, Taiwan's new ruler, the government of the Republic of China, instituted a policy called the Movement to Improve Aboriginal People's Lifestyle, which completely altered the traditional life in the mountain forest.

This "improved" lifestyle, like that encouraged by the Japanese, called for the Taiwanese mountain people to use money to purchase their daily products from merchants who sold these goods at a profit. As a result, the aboriginals were forced to give up all the free, natural supplies that were readily available in or a stone's throw from their own house. Instead, they now had to figure out who bought what farm products when and where, and then carry whatever they had on their backs for hours to the nearest store in order to sell it to them. In exchange, the mountain people purchased and brought back home a variety of industrial products, including the stuff called soap.

Here was the problem. Adults worked in the forest or rice field all day long, and kids played like naughty monkeys all day too; their dirty clothes would easily use up a bar of soap in three or four days, even if the soap was used frugally. For that, our *amo* (father) would often grumble, blaming us, the nonproductive kids who didn't know how to treat our clothes well and keep them clean, while also blaming the family member who washed the clothes for not using soap sparingly!

Later, a product called Non-soap Powder (like today's laundry powder) became available in our village. Just a teaspoon of the powder could make a lot of bubbles. How amazing! A package of the powder cost several times what a bar of soap would cost. Families that bought this stuff appeared different and seemed to be of a higher social status than other families, and were admired by the people unfamiliar with industrial products.

On the other hand, my *ak'i* (grandfather) would never use soap or non-soap products; he would always use traditional cleaning products. He didn't have any interest in soaps that cost money to purchase.

As I remember, among the cleaning products Ak'i used, the one he used the most was camellia seed solution. Ripe camellia seeds were crushed first and then put in water. The water solution was then used to wash hair, clothes, bathe, etc. It was also good for hair and skin.

My *ino* (mother) also washed her hair with camellia seed solution, and her hair always looked soft and shinning. We ignorant sisters, however, always used purchased soap to take baths, wash our faces, and so forth—a result of looking down on our ancestors' ways and wisdom, worshiping industrial products instead. These products seriously damaged our hair, making it dry, split at the end, and easy to break. Thinking back now, I feel sorry for ourselves for having been so ignorant.

In addition to camellia seeds, we also used soapberry seeds collected from the forests. The seeds, if not examined closely, could be mistaken as shell-removed dried longans with a pit, because they are about the same size. Remove the flesh that covers the seed, and scrub the flesh in water. Bright white bubbles appear and can be used for bathing, and for washing hair and clothes.

Under the most deprived circumstances, when neither camellia seeds nor soapberry seeds were available, the last resort was to use fire ash from under the stove. For washing clothes, we would put fire ash in the water for at least overnight, so that it would release alkaline into the water to make a coffee-colored alkaline solution that had powerful cleansing effects. Fire ash could also be used directly for cleansing kitchen utensils to remove grease, and to make aluminum-made utensils clean and shine.

Years after worshiping industrial products, I am aware of how they can be harmful to the environment. All of these "modern improvements" make me miss my *ak'i* and his use of natural cleansers.

Paiz's Remembrance of Her Homeland[56]

By Dr. Tai-Li Hu (胡台麗博士)[57]

More than two years ago, I was reviewing articles submitted to the essay division of the "1999 First Competition of the Aboriginal Literature," sponsored by the Chung-Hwa Automobile Co. I still remember vividly an article I read titled *Wood Clogs.* The author was a Tsou (鄒族) woman who was approaching retirement age. She described hearing the sound of *"ko, ko, ko, ko ..."* while she was on the streets in Hsin-Chuang (新莊), shopping to prepare for the arrival of the Lunar New Year; that sound brought back her memories of childhood living in her homeland. As a *putu* (漢人, a Han ethnic Chinese in the Tsou language) having visited the Tsou tribe in Alishan (阿里山) a few times, I read this article with a feeling of exhilaration and could all but experience physically the atmosphere of this pristine, refreshing, and rustic environment as she described it.

Through the eyes of the curious and sensitive young girl, we could "see" some Han people arriving at the mountainous land of the Tsou's—at a time when Taiwan was ruled by the Japanese—to negotiate with her father the business of cutting down some of his *putu* trees, a kind of tree introduced by ethnic Han people that bears their name, in order to make wood clogs. *Putu* trees are the trees that blossom in early summer with white flowers, making the moun-

---

56. *This preface originally appeared in the book's Chinese edition, published in 2003.*
57. *Dr. Tai-Li Hu is a Distinguished Research Fellow and the Director at the Institute of Ethnology, Academia Sinica, Taiwan.*

tains look like an ocean full of white waves! Even though the little girl sympathized with the hard-working *putus*, and realized that her *amo* (father) needed the income to build a new family house, her young, innocent heart couldn't help but mourn the disappearance of the beautiful white waves. But the author doesn't trap herself in any ideological box; rather, with gentleness and sincerity she touches upon varied subjects facing ethnic minorities: the actual living situations, historic transitions, and contacts with other groups of ethnic minorities—all in such a way that leaves you, the reader, with lingering afterthoughts. Later, I saw her dressed up in a traditional Tsou costume at the essay award ceremony, sitting on the stage as quiet as the fairytale mountain she had written about in her stories and seemed to have brought along with her. I had been hoping that she would write more stories of her homeland. Well, here you are, the book *My Dear Ak'i, Please Don't Be Upset.*

It is my impression that authors today in Taiwan who are aboriginal by ethnicity and who write about native Taiwanese stories, legends, and other topics are predominately post-World War II urban and educated young men. Their more lively and diverse living experiences are far different from those of the author Paiz[58], who was born in the early 1940s and grew up in a geographically remote and pristine environment, and has retained strong and flavorful memories of it.

We should be grateful to Ms. Hsin-I Tseng (曾心儀), a writing teacher at the Hsin-Chuang Community College (新莊社大) in Taipei County, Taiwan, who recognized Paiz's natural writing talent and proceeded

---

58. *This preface was written in 2003, when the author was still known as Paiz Mukunana.*

to provide her with instruction and encouragement. As a result, the author, a housewife married to a *putu*, who lives in Northern Taiwan and who by ethnicity is Tsou, continues to write about her cherished homeland memories. Thanks also to Taiwan Indigenous Voice Publishing House (山海文化雜誌社), and Fembooks Publishing House (女書店). Both show great interest in the work of female and Taiwanese aboriginal writers. Due to their dedicated support, Paiz's writings can be shared with the public.

In writing the memories of her childhood homeland, the author exhibits a deep sense of loss that can't be easily compensated. "Borrowing a writing system from another culture to recount the Tsou's history and events somehow gives me the feeling that something is missing—some special, subtle flavor; something that only we Tsou people could smell and tell." For Taiwan's aboriginal ethnic groups who don't have their own writing systems, the spoken word remains the sole means of communication at their disposal, and is as important to them as their own flesh and blood. In converting the oral histories of people, places, and events into the written words of a different ethnic group, certain subtleties found in the spoken original cannot always be adequately expressed. However, Paiz's effort is eye-opening. She uses simple, effortless-yet-eloquent colloquial words in order to transport us to an ancient but still existent Tsou wonderland of rivers, mountains, and vegetation—one that has all but been forgotten—and to enable us to feel the apprehension of Tsou's younger generations in contemporary society.

According to legend, the Tsou people in the author's stories were created by Hamo (天神), the supreme God, and scattered in Tsou Head and Branch Communities.[59] For their part, the native people have continuously practiced rituals to express their gratitude and to say prayers to the gods of heaven, earth, mountains, rivers, crops, plants, etc. In the past, the Tsou followed traditional customs for child births, marriages, and burials. For example, the spirits of the dead went back to Hohcʉbʉ (塔山, Pagoda Mountain), and the body of the diseased was buried inside the family house in a squatting posture. There was no need to erect a tombstone, which meant that neither they or future generations were required to perform annual tombstone sweeping. However, in comparison to the culture of the *putu* which emphasized ancestor worship at home and at the grave site, Paiz and her relatives of the following two generations, who grew up outside the Tsou communities, experienced great anxiety while searching for their traditions; they were not able to even find their ancestors' grave sites. For those younger generations that succeeded her, who can't speak the Tsou's mother tongue, being able to locate and sweep the ancestors' graves as the *putus* did during the *putu's* Tombstone Sweeping Festival, and to have a family genealogy as the *putus* did, helped fill some of the void left by an absence of their own traditions. No wonder Paiz wanted to say: "My dear Ak'i, please don't be upset."

Every episode Paiz relates about experiences in her homeland seems to be accompanied with a faint sigh. On the one hand, she presents to us the natural, beautiful, and rich colors and tastes of pristine forest and wilderness; on the other hand, she conveys a difficult life of endless labor and hardship accompanied by the shortage

---

59. *Historically the chief of the head community was in charge of the branch communities; they were blessed and protected by* ba'eton'u *[粟女神之名, the name of Goddess Millet] and* i'afafeoi *[戰神, Warrior God].*

of daily commodities. Being an avid eater like Paiz, I was particularly interested in the stories in which she describes picking natural snacks in the wilderness. Sugar and salt were once extremely scarce in the remote mountain regions of Taiwan. Children of the Tsou, however, were able to pick their own natural vegetable snacks in the wilderness, to taste and savor their sweetness and saltiness, and to share the enjoyment with others. As an example, in her story *Memories of Bees*, Paiz mentions how the honey bees extract pollen from the wild chrysanthemum flowers, and turn the pollen into shiny, beautifully tender, yellow-colored honey which releases its fragrance into the surrounding air. In the story *Our Natural Brand of Chewing Gum*, she notes how the sticky, sweet, and fragrant *kupiya* nut flesh could be blown into bubbles; how silver grass roots and the defectively-grown white fruits on camellia trees tasted unforgettably sweet, clear, and cool; and how by licking the fruits of the roxbourgh sumac their salty taste came alive.

Other than snacks from the wilderness, acquisition of staple foods required a lot of labor. Paiz recounts the grueling process of farming millet, in a narrative that proves quite interesting indeed. After scorching a piece of land for farming, she explains, the resulting ash from the silver grass bush makes the farm workers look like "the dark-skinned person in the toothpaste ads."[60] Or this: While in charge of scaring birds away from the crops by yanking on a bird-scaring device, children never forgot to find time to wander off and pick wild strawberries. When her father was spearing fish one night at a section of the river that had been allocated to her family, Paiz, who carried a torch for

---

60. *Back then, there was a toothpaste brand called* Darkie Toothpaste *(*黑人牙膏*). (See note #43.)*

him, lay down upon on a big rock to watch the stars in the sky.

As a female author, Paiz wrote two articles on women in the labor force. In *Labor Exchange Co-operative,* she explains that unmarried young ladies in the remote mountains, where they were isolated, "didn't have to behave lady-like; instead, we laughed out loud, and fearlessly announced our personal secrets—nothing was off limit. Even though the work was hard, we were happy girls. In *'Tis the Season to Harvest Palm Fiber Sheaths,* the author, at a young age, accompanied her widowed second aunt to the deep mountains to harvest palm sheaths; they did this for the income, so that her aunt could financially support her two sons who were studying in a far-away city. Alone in the wilderness, the woman and young girl built a temporary shelter, made fires with dry wood for cooking, and stayed there for six or seven days. Paiz says she learned from experience that "during these tough economic times, exhaustion from physically demanding work was common; it was really a way of life." Fortunately, her aunt sold the palm sheaths at a very good price, which later enabled her son to bring home the first camera owned by anyone in the entire village. Another heart-felt but comical story about selling dried plants had its origins at the author's elementary school. The principal encouraged the students to take advantage of outdoor class time to gather mesona grass from the mountains, and then dry and sell it. The income from the sale was used to make new uniforms for students who otherwise wore shabby and sometimes ragged clothes.

Paiz, like many other young women growing up in the remote mountains, or anywhere else, loved beauty. Towards this end, and detailed in a piece she writes titled *My Hair Stories,* she curled her hair, transforming herself from a no-makeup little girl to a glamorous young lady. While at a later age she was to leave the Tsou community to live in the *putu* community, the author's memories of her homeland would always stay with her, and deepen with the passage of time. Finally, against all odds—by fate or just plain luck—Paiz wrote this, her first book! In the early morning sun, the book sparkles with dew drops, mixed with crystal clear tear drops saturated with the deep affection of the Tsou woman longing for her homeland.

My Encounter with Lady Alishan[61]

By Ms. Hsin-I Tseng (曾心儀女士)

I have been involved in numerous political activities related to Taiwan's democratic movement. As a result, I have known a few aboriginals, although not in close relationship. People who are in democratic movements in general have tight schedules; they meet and depart right after a meeting or activity. It can be said that Paiz is the first Taiwanese aboriginal that I have developed a close and sincere friendship with. Her Mandarin Chinese name is Shiang-Mei (香梅), and her name in the Tsou language is Paiz Mʉkʉnana.[62]

When I walked for the first time into a classroom at an evening school for adult continuing education, to teach my first class in *Novel Writing,* my heart was pounding because the class size was very small, fewer than ten. Shiang-Mei joined my class two or three weeks after the semester began. She was a middle-aged woman; her face showed signs of someone who had gone through numerous complex and challenging life experiences. She appeared calm and reserved. Anyone in the class, I believed, could tell at first glance that she was an aboriginal woman. While certain facial characteristics may make a person appear to be of a different race, it's not so easy to describe exactly what these physical differences are.

The students introduced themselves and chatted among them-

---

61. *This preface originally appeared in the Chinese edition of the book, published in 2003.*
62. *When this article was written, the author was still known as Paiz Mʉkʉnana.*

selves. Shiang-Mei in no time let everyone know that she was a Tsou tribal member from Alishan (阿里山), and explained that it had been a long time since she left the tribal land. She said that nowadays her homeland was very different from the way it was, that today it was rather similar to the rest of Taiwan. Upon hearing what she said, I could not imagine what the Tsou tribal community was like in the past.

The school where I was teaching was located in Taipei County. The continuing education program was founded by a group who promoted education reform, and the lectures took place in a borrowed space at a local provincial high school. In my novel writing class, I encouraged students to write about their personal experiences and feelings, especially those connected to the "921 Earthquake" that took place not long ago.[63] Shiang-Mei also wrote an article relating to the earthquake, in which the primary figure was a man who took an early morning walk to the earthquake calamity site to pay tribute to the dead. I was amazed by her narration, which, unlike the other students', didn't make use of the first person perspective but rather the third. Even though her writing style was not yet fluent, her potential clearly was emerging. From the beginning, I made up my mind to encourage her, to help her cultivate a skill that leaned toward writing articles relating to aboriginal literature, and to do this while following her own path formed by her unique life experiences.

Following that first article, the subsequent ones surprised me immensely. It can be said that the first article was the beginning of the remarkable writing career of this Tsou woman. It was very clear

---

63. *On September 21, 1999, there was a catastrophic earthquake in central Taiwan. More than 2,400 people lost their lives, and more than 11,000 people were injured.*

to me that she had said goodbye to her previous period of writing; in terms of writing style, creativity, and vision she would no longer be like duckweed—a ubiquitous and aggressive free-floating pond plant— inhabiting the waters of literary sameness shared by many mainstream writers in the Han society.

When she handed me her first piece, which dealt with indigenous women working in the mountains, I felt while reading as though my hands were burning. It was the first time I realized that the Taiwanese aboriginals were full of vitality and happiness, and enjoyed immensely their lives in the mountains. To me the impressions I held—of these people working, playing, and living together—were not unlike beautiful scenes from a story in ancient mythology. As explained in the article, due to the great distance between their houses and their working sites, Shiang-Mei and her aunt were forced to spend days in the deep mountains in order to harvest palm sheaths. They built temporary sheds in which to sleep at night. They made fires for cooking, boiling water, heating up the shed, and for fending off wild animals—using whatever materials were at hand. They truly worked and slept in the wild. Being fatigued and falling asleep quickly at dusk were probably the reasons why Shiang-Mei didn't provide us with more details about her nights there.

Without a doubt her writing is smooth, her choice of words impeccable. It helped that she was a quick learner. Shiang-Mei was married at a young age to an army lieutenant from mainland China, whose military duties involved office work. It is reasonable to assume that he may have had a strong impact on her learning to speak and write Chinese. I surmise that she could master the language of any country she might live in, be it French, Japanese, or English. She is extremely sharp, excelling in whatever subject is at hand. While other middle-age people may hesitate to learn how to use computers, Shiang-Mei learned in a few days, and handed me her work which she had successfully typed on a computer. She learned how to play the piano so that she could serve as an accompanist in a church. She learned things fast, including riding a motorcycle and driving a car.

When I received her first essay on aboriginal culture, I was pleasantly surprised, and excited by my belief that she had created an important piece of literature for Taiwan. I was sure were she to continue to write, she would meet with great success.

I reminded myself: protect and take care of her; while working with her, don't let her fall into short-sighted, profit-minded traps. In other words, do not let her writings be used for reasons of pride or vanity. I knew that she would appear attractive to the publication industry, and that they might take advantage of her as a commercial object for profit-making purposes. After all, her voice was unique and cutting edge in its exploration of aboriginal culture. They might encourage her to write popular stories that didn't reflect her natural honesty and virtue, that were instead designed to falsely boost her popularity— and sales—while garnering her literary fame for all the wrong reasons. Also, I wouldn't want to personally benefit from having a famous writing student. With an eye towards the future, I desired to make certain that Shiang-Mei would continue to develop and polish her own writing style, and become a "solid" writer working on projects that were not only good for her career but for the culture of her indigenous people.

When I read the second article Shiang-Mei handed me, on her experiences living in the mountains, I began to cry after just a few lines. She depicts the hardships of life, how the students and their parents did everything they could to appease the teachers, who came from the "plains," [64] so they would stay in the mountains and teach; their turnover rate was very high.[65] In addition to being shocked by this episode, I was also shocked, as if struck by lightning, when I read the unexpected conclusion to her well-orchestrated story: The school principal led the students on a trek to gather mesona grass from the mountains in order to purchase new uniforms for them, the first uniforms the kids had ever had.

Shiang-Mei describes things and events delicately, vividly, and with emotion; her stories left deep impressions in my mind, occurring as they did in that far off fairyland so close to heaven. Although their lives were full of hardship (e.g., poverty, disease, lack of daily commodities, and more), she reveals to the reader the remarkably rich and precious core values these aboriginals nonetheless hold dear—a belief system that we, living in the plains, find alien today. Alas, these precious things are vanishing, along with the disappearance of the indigenous people themselves—a situation that makes me cry. What I can do about it is rather limited, I can only do my best to help my student develop and realize her writing potential.

In a classroom discussion, Shiang-Mei noted that the annual *Mayasbi* (Warrior Festival) was the most representative of all Tsou cultural activities. Since the festival for that year had already passed, I told her that I wished to attend the annual *Mayasbi* the following year. This

---

64. *When the Han population was growing, a gradual process that began some 400 to 500 years ago, most of them lived in the plains land. Over time, Han people came to be called "plains people" and the aboriginals were called "mountain people," because most of them lived in the mountains.*

65. *Because the living conditions were difficult in the aboriginal regions, teachers from the "plains" rarely stayed in the mountains for long.*

was the first time Shiang-Mei and I talked about it; previously I knew nothing about the festival. She said that when the time came, I could join a tourist group for the event, and that she could arrange my overnight stay at her relatives' residence as there were no hotels nearby.

Shiang-Mei continued to write, both qualitatively and quantitatively. She wrote about her father building the family house (her father was very good at carving stones into various shapes, work far more intricate and demanding than paving the ground for the stone sign used at the school's gate). She wrote about the merchants from the plains who came to the mountains to cut trees for making wood clogs; about gathering honey from honeycombs on the way to and back from school, and about how hard her aunt worked to raise funds to mail to her children to pay for their school tuition. In addition, she had started to write articles on Tsou traditions and folk stories. According to the legends, the Tsou people originated from the Jade Mountain, then moved down to the Alishan area; accompanied by other peoples, they also moved to different areas in Taiwan, such as the Tao-yuan and Shan-ming villages in Kaohsiung County. Presently, most of the Tsou people remain concentrated in Alishan. The overall population of the Tsou people today is about 6,000,[66] with most of them scattered in the mountain ranges.

Seeing Shiang-Mei write such moving articles, one after the other, gave me a feeling of having achieved a major lifetime accomplishment of my own. I was so proud. Over two semesters, the number of articles she handed me was enough to put together for a book. When I heard there was a request for articles for an aboriginal writing competition, I encouraged her to participate in the event, and suggested that she sub-

---

66. *As of 2018, the Tsou population was about 6,000.*

mit the article titled *Wood Clogs*, the story about Han wood-clog makers who had a contract with her family to cut trees to make the clogs. She hesitated and hesitated, and took no action for a long time. When the closing date was near, she finally submitted the article—but not before my constant entreaties.

After a period of time, one day I accidentally read about the competition results in a newspaper, and saw her name on the award list. I jumped and screamed out of happiness! I made a point to attend the award ceremony, and saw all of the award recipients in their respective tribal costumes. They looked beautiful and dignified, majestic and magnificent, as in a wonderland! How I was moved! But I was somewhat confused: Was it all real or imaginary?

Before me were the award recipients and their tribal people. As if they had returned to their own tribal communities, they exhibited their true selves—selves that had been suppressed and forgotten. When they spoke on the stage, they all lamented openly the pain they experienced facing the disappearance of their tribe. Tears were shed on and off the stage. Today, they were the major characters of the article competition event. There were also honored guests who were invited to represent the government. One might therefore assume that the aborigines' plights were being heard. However, I was still afraid of the realities they might face when the event was over. Would their fragile hopes and struggles be buried again by a worldly society concerned mostly with values that were secular and utilitarian?

Before the end of the third semester, Shiang-Mei told us that the Warrior Festival for the year would be held on February 15th. Because the plan of having a touring group attend the event fell apart, Shiang-

Mei said that if I wanted to attend the festival, she would give me a ride. I accepted her offer, and would stay at her house the night before the trip. At her home that evening, I was in a hurry to get myself ready; due to my other involvements during that period, I didn't have much time to prepare myself for the trip. Hurriedly, I picked up my traveling bag, down coat, handbag, and snack box, and rushed out to catch a taxi, at close to eleven o'clock at night. I wasn't excited and didn't enjoy the drive; rather, I felt perturbed by my having troubled Shiang-Mei.

Shiang-Mei had entertained classmates with dinners at her house before; they were extremely impressed by the cleanliness and warmth of her home. That evening, I was the sole guest, and was honored to be there. She led me to the guest room upstairs. To my surprise, she still had the energy to chat with me until the wee hours. This relaxed me somewhat—I no longer felt so perturbed—and our time together enabled me to enjoy our friendship. While chatting, she showed me a new book she had just purchased, written by a famous actress named Lan-hwa Tang (湯蘭花). I didn't know until then that Tang was also a Tsou tribal member. In her biography, Tang described having married a business man, being implicated in her husband's debt and bankruptcy, and putting in extra hours in the show business to make more money to pay back her husband's debt. She wrote also of her fugitive life, and her efforts to avoid being caught and put in prison; her husband had written checks under her name. Alas, the amount of debt was bottom-less. Being a fugitive, she could not go home. Finally, she decided to divorce him and managed to create a new life of her own.

We left Shiang-Mei's house at six the following morning. For the next few days she drove from dawn to dusk. I was very impressed by her will and energy. Along the way, she pointed out a mountain ridge and explained to me that she and her people used to walk from one side of the mountain to the other, often without wearing shoes because shoes were hard to come by. She said they often picked the straightest, shortest path—as the crow flies—because there were no trails. While healthy people could manage that kind of trek, a sick person would be carried on the back of a family member, sometimes in a basket. Gazing at mountain after mountain, and the steep cliffs scattered here and there, chills would run up and down my spine. At the same time I would be thinking: "I'm afraid I would never be able to even make one trip like that!"

Shiang-Mei also told me that, in an article of hers, she described a devoted husband carrying his sick wife on his back in a basket, walking up and down the mountains to get to a doctor's office. She said it was a true story, and added that, alas, both of them had since passed away. While here in the mountains, my inner heart pounded fiercely in response to the vast discrepancy between rural and urban areas when it came to infrastructure and available medical resources. The plight of these aboriginal people—and their courage and spirit—was further illustrated by the manifestation of the heroic husband's oath upon marriage to take care of his wife for life.

Driving skillfully along winding roads surrounded by endless mountains, Shiang-Mei behaved like a fearless female warrior who knew the terrain and that nothing could stop her. She was so familiar with the environment—her childhood kingdom— it was as though she were relying on, more than sight, her sense of smell to find her youthful footprints: the haunts of her past, her memories of the mountains through which she had so happily galloped. She told me that when she was attending the elementary school, it took her one hour to walk to school and another hour to return home; it took even longer for some of her classmates. I was amused when she said that while driving, a car had to follow a winding mountain road, but while walking to school, they followed a path that ran straight down from the top of a mountain. The latter mode of transportation was much faster, she said.

Shiang-Mei took me to visit the Danayiku Ecology Park (達娜伊谷自然生態公園) in Shanmei Village (山美村), or *Saviki* in the Tsou language, which has a population of about 600; the Park is run by the Shanmei Community Development Association (山美社區發展協會). The Park's most significant feature is its fish ponds, found in the natural environment of the mountains. You can see running water in the mountain brooks, small ponds here and there in the valleys, and fish swimming freely—a scene that had me shouting with joy! The day we were visiting wasn't a holiday, which meant the entire village was quiet. According to some local villagers, if it had been a holiday the entire place would have been crowded with visitors. There was a vending area by the park entrance, where one vendor sold smoked pork that he made using a huge, circular meat smoker with a fire underneath. Pieces of pork hung from the device, which emitted a tremendous amount of smoke, while an aromatic smell permeated the air. We were told by the villagers that visitors could stay overnight at cabins nearby. We visited the cabins, and saw that the building designs were rather avant garde. There was a beautiful garden nearby, with a plum blossom that was just gorgeous. It was obvious that were there to be sufficient funds available to develop this area, the future of tourism here would be very bright.

That evening, we were invited for dinner by Shiang-Mei's eldest niece, Shiao-Lin. I was told that as the Warrior Festival approached, each household prepared abundant food in order to entertain tribal friends, and their own family members who lived in outside communities and returned to attend the festival. It was not unusual to see several dozen guests at one dinner table. Something I found unique here was that each house was built on high ground; Shiao-Lin's house was no exception. We climbed slopes all of the time.

The first sight of Shiao-Lin was eye-opening! She was so natural, so glowing in spirit as if she were part of the surrounding mountains! Even though she was small and slender physically, spiritually she was powerful and full of energy—so much so that I felt she was like a gem in the deep mountains that hadn't been discovered let alone carved upon. It was my hope that she would remain the way she was. I watched her busily preparing the meal, helped by a few women neighbors. Laughing, she said, "Every thing is free for this meal. We grow our own vegetables, raise chickens, catch fish in the river." Then she pointed to the water faucet in the kitchen. "And water is available from the mountains all year round, free of charge." The mountain people used natural gas canisters for cooking—turned up high when stir-frying. Every dish was huge. It was a very delicious meal, especially the vegetable dishes: cabbage, pumpkin, and chayote (a kind of squash), they all tasted fresh, sweet, and tender. I felt that we were here in the fairyland, and ate what fairies ate.

While we were happily eating, Shiao-Lin's husband returned from a trip. He had taken a relative with a farming tractor, on the tractor, to see a doctor in the plains. Even though money was not easy to come by, the couple had tried all means to save money to purchase the vehicle. Not having a vehicle in this mountainous country would make it very difficult to compete for odd jobs in order to make a living. When parents went to work, their young children stayed home and took care of themselves. I had heard that kids as young as primary schoolers knew how to operate their fathers' farming tractors. Because the kids were still so short, they would have to stand up to run the vehicle.

Before we arrived at the site of this year's Warrior Festival, Shiang-Mei took me to visit the most populous township in Alishan—Tapangʉ (達邦 Dar-ban) Village. There, one could find everything from the Village Office, Office of Village Representatives, local police station, Office of Farming, and a hospital (more of a medical clinic really, the only one of its kind in quite a vast area), library, athletic competition fields, etc. We saw a villager carrying a sick relative on his back, step by step into the clinic. If people didn't have a vehicle, that's what they had to do to bring someone in for medical treatment. On this trip, this particular experience was the saddest thing to me. Astronauts had walked on the Moon, satellites and space stations flew over our heads regularly; yet, the aborigines still needed to use their feet to carry seriously ill persons up and down many mountains to find emergency medical treatment!

This year's Warrior Festival was held in Tfuya (特富野部落), which belonged to Tapangʉ Village (達邦村). If viewed from a much higher site, Tfuya appeared to be situated on a small, flat platform on a hill. However, when one stood on the festival ground of Tfuya, one felt the sky wasn't too far overhead, and that the festival that was held to entertain the fairies was right in front of their residence! As for the surrounding mountains, they were like folding screens in their living rooms.

The entrance to the festival was decorated modestly, yet beautifully. Freshly collected bright-green grass leaves were used to wrap the columns of the archway. On the top of the archway, the horizontal board displayed "2001 Mayasbi Festival, Tfuya, Alishan" in red on a white background. Romanization, or Latinization, of the event name was also displayed along with the Mandarin Chinese. Simple aboriginal drawings were also part of the decorations.

Tsou people who returned here to participate in the festival dressed in their traditional costume. Some of the members who didn't dress up completely might wear a vest, a traditional hat, or other headwear. We met a Tsou council member who told us that he was going to wear a bear-fur cap that displayed a chunk of white fur surrounded by black fur. The look was meant to symbolize something rare and important: the man himself, in his role as council member, who was now easily identifiable in a crowd. The Tsou's costumes and decorations, for both men and women, were very bright in color, and lively and cheerful. Many families came back to the village in vehicles, all kinds of vehicles: sedans, trucks, tractors, motorcycles. Once there, many elders couldn't move around easily without assistance from their children or grandchildren.

This time, when Shiang-Mei returned to her village, she had a very hectic schedule and found it wasn't easy finding time for everyone. Nonetheless, she was very affectionate towards and thoughtful of her relatives who still lived here. She gave presents to the elderly ones, and chatted with them. On our way to the festival, she visited an old woman who lived alone, and offered her a ride to the festival. This elderly woman still did her own farming, and grew all kinds of things, like vegetables, which surrounded her house. Her husband had died and her children lived in other communities, where they had jobs. Although she was rather old and one of her legs had problems, this woman was still very spirited. She said that some time ago she fell and broke her leg. After the fractures healed, unfortunately her leg couldn't bend. When she was boarding a vehicle, she would laboriously pull her leg with her hands into the vehicle. Because of her condition, she rarely left the house unless she needed to go to the city; in that case, she would walk to the road by her farm, and wait for someone who was willing to offer her a ride to a bus station, some distance away.

In this tribal community, there were many cases like this woman's. It has to do with medical care and physical therapy. Alas, as noted there is a severe shortage of medical facilities, depriving the injured the opportunity for proper recovery, a regret they will carry with them for the rest of their lives. These people are also more likely to suffer from other accidents and related medical problems due to their poor physical coordination.

Owing to their daily physical work in the mountains, almost all of the aboriginals, men or women, develop solid feet and strong hands, and because they use both a lot more than other people might, they are subject to frequent injuries. Their feet and hands, injured or sound, have become popular subjects for artists, inspiring the painters to create drawings and paintings featuring them. Of course, in the indigenous environment there are boundless art subjects that are beautiful, moving, overpowering, inspiring. These include mountain landscapes, people at work and play, animals, vegetation, buildings, illustrated folk tales, and other treasures for the artistic eye.

The *Kuba,* or Men's Meeting Place, is a unique feature of Tsou culture. Women are not allowed to enter the building. It has always been this way, even up to today. Shiang-Mei and I were running on foot down from the mountain to catch the opening of the annual festival. Before it started, several strong warriors planted new divine flowers, like those that were planted the previous year, on the ridge of the *kuba* roof. There were limited seats for the guests; many festival participants had to crowd together by the stone fence on the slope near the road, away from the festival square. It was extremely hot that day—the festival was scheduled for 10:00 a.m. to 12:00 noon—and visitors from all over brought their own cameras and camcorders to capture the event.

It was inevitable that government officials were invited to address the crowd. After the change of the Taiwan presidential administration,[67] most of the officials were DPP members. It was very clear that politics weighed heavily on local affairs. Most of the officials were there on behalf of the heads of some higher office branches, which made me wonder whether the new government had a genuine interest in aboriginal affairs.

The festival got underway, with warriors carrying the torch from inside the *kuba* to the center of the square, where they gestured to the almighty gods. Then, all of the participating men walked to the divine tree. They knifed a baby pig; each blotted their sword with the blood and raised it in front of the divine tree. They howled while wiping their swords against the tree, to let the warrior god know that the festival had begun.

Next was the trimming of the branches of the divine tree, one of the festival's most interesting and symbolic actions. They left three, creating a path for the gods while symbolizing that life was renewed. The gods descended using these divine-tree branches as a sky ladder, all the way down to the square where they would enjoy the offering that had been prepared for them. As the ritual progressed, the *peongsi*

---

67. *From 1945 to 2000, Taiwan was governed by the Kuomingtang (KMT) Party and, therefore, the presidents were all KMT members. In 2000, the opposition party, the Democratic Progressive Party (DPP), won the election and Mr. Shui-bian Chen became the president.*

(chief) twice led the elders and the young warriors in the singing of the "inviting song," asking that the gods join them. The song was very moving because of its simplicity. Later, women joined the ritual. They carried torches and placed them into the fire pit, and also participated in the dancing troupe.

It was my great fortune to take part in the Warrior Festival in Alishan! Deeply in my heart, I feel that different groups of people have their own culture, different life styles, and that to understand each other it takes personal participation in other people's living experiences. It takes respect for outsiders to establish a basis for fundamental mutual understanding. I have a rather uneasy feeling knowing that I have waited so long to take the first step regarding my own participation in the Tsou people's activities. On the other hand, I am fortunate to have the opportunity—an opportunity that many people may never have in their entire lives.

Shiang-Mei indeed is a wonderful Tsou woman. She took me to the wilderness, pointing at a mountain that was full of grass, and another that was full of cliffs, where there were footprints—traces, evidence—of the life and struggles of her tribal people. She wasn't afraid of the rugged, often treacherous mountains. She never forgot the homeland where she grew up, and which she missed more with each passing year. I have noticed the burning desire and anxiousness in her eyes to record the gradually disappearing life of her tribal culture.

My encounter and association with Shiang-Mei remains such a wonderful page in my life! It was a blank page at first, but gradually, as our relationship deepened, it filled with rich content that I believe for us portends a bright and promising future.

Appendix

Glossary of Terms
Terms in the Tsou Language, Written Mandarin Chinese, and Pronunciation of Written Mandarin Chinese
(Inside the parentheses is the English translation, or explanation)

Romanization in Tsou Language	Written Mandarin Chinese	English Pronunciation or Translation of Written Chinese
amo	父親	(father)
Amo Hamo	天神哈莫	(Supreme God Hamo)
amoconi	叔父	(uncle)
Atuhcu c'oeha	曾文溪	(Tseng-Wen River)
Atuhcu Hohcubu	大塔山	Da-Tar Shan (Large Pagoda Mountain)
Ba'eton''u	粟女神，小米女神	(Goddess Millet)
Cayamavana	茶山	Char-Shan (name of a mountain)
Ciingona ta Hohcubu	小塔山	Siao-Tar Shan (Small Pagoda Mountain)
c'oeha	河川	(river, brook, stream)
C'oeha no m'okvou	陳有蘭溪	(Chen-You-Lan River)
Danayiku Ecology Park	達娜伊谷自然生態公園	(Danayiku Ecology Park)
fifiho	（新郎對女方家提供的工作義務）	(groom's labor commitment to the bride's maiden family)
Hohcubu	塔山	Tar Shan (Pagoda Mountain)
Homeyaya	豐年祭	(Harvest Festival)
Hosa	大社	(Head Community)
hosa tapangu	達邦社	Da-Bang Sher (Da-Bang Head Community)
hupa	獵場	(hunting ground)
ino	母親	(mother)

Kuba	男人會所	(Men's Meeting Place)
Lalauya	樂野	Ler-Yie (name of a village)
Lenohi'u	小社	(Branch Community)
maaseu	網撈法	(fishing with a net)
Maeno	霞山	Shia-Shan (name of a mountain)
Mayasbi	戰祭	(Warrior Festival)
Nivnu	尼弗奴 (粟女神的名字)	(name of Goddess Millet)
Oi'iana	新美	Shin-Mei (name of a village)
otfo	毒魚法	(fishing with poison)
Patunkuonu	玉山，八通關	(Mt. Jade)
Peongsi	頭目	Tou-moo (in Mandarin Chinese, meaning "Chief")
Psaseongana	阿里山	Alishan (Mt. Ali)
putu	漢人	(a Han person)
putunoapihana	台海另一邊的漢人	(a Han person from the other side of the Taiwan Strait)
Saviki	山美	Shan-Mei (name of a village)
Seya'funu	石	Sih-Tsou (name of a village)
siiungu	魚槺法	(a fishing method)
ta'eucu	山藥薯	(Asian mountain yam)
Takezaki	竹崎	Zu-Chee (name of a village)
Tataka	塔塔加	Tatagia (an area of Mt. Jade)
Tapangu	達邦	Dar-Bang (name of a village)
Tfuya	特富野部落	Ter-fu-ye Community
toa'lungu	垂釣法	(fishing with a hook and line)
Toeku	長谷川	Chang-Gu River
ton'u	粟	(millet)
tufngi	叉魚法	(fish spearing)
T'ut'ubuhu	水山	Shuei-Shan (name of a village)
tu'u	小鐵鏟	(adze)
va'ahu	山澗小溪	(small river, brook)
Vokudana	弗古達那	(name of a river)
Yayoveya	亞有彿亞	(the valley where *Mukⱨnana* ancestors settled)
Yiskiana	伊西基阿那溪	(name of a river)

About the Author

Born in the Lalauya Community in 1942, Faisʉ Mʉkʉnana has lived through two regimes—the Japanese colonialist government and the Republic of China (Taiwan)—and learned three languages: her tribal Tsou, Japanese, and Mandarin. Her unusual life experience has greatly nourished her literary career, and the rich native cultural heritage she has inherited is a boundless resource for her engaging and compelling writing.

Faisʉ Mʉkʉnana is the recipient of several significant literary awards in Taiwan, including Taiwan Indigenous Literature Competition Award. Most recently (in 2017), she published *Ancestral Faces in the Glow of Fire* (by Taiwan Indigenous Voice Publishing House). She is one of the most acclaimed Taiwanese indigenous writers.

The author lives in Taipei with her husband, a retired military officer. In addition to writing, she is actively involved in aboriginal affairs in Taiwan.

About the Translator

Yao-Chung Tsao was born and raised in Taipei, Taiwan, before moving to and studying in the U.S. in 1969. He was on the faculty at Rensselaer Polytechnic Institute in New York State, and later joined AT&T Bell Labs in New Jersey.

Born in the same year as the author, as a youngster he spent many years in remote mountain villages, having experiences similar to the author's. As a human cognition psychologist and an industrial engineer by training, he is especially sensitive to the social, cultural, racial, and political issues in Taiwan. He appreciates that Faisu Mukunana's stories touch upon these issues, and do so in a humorous yet subtle manner and through a writing style that invites further explorations by curious minds.

In addition to translating, Yao enjoys painting and sings with a community chorale in New Jersey, not far from his home where he lives with his wife, also from Taiwan.

About the Editor

Cort Smith, an award-winning writer and editor, was born in Manhattan and grew up near the Jersey Shore. His professional background encompasses more than 35 years in publishing and related industries, with achievements in the areas of feature/news writing, editing, copy writing, marketing, public relations, and management. He received his early training—and worldview influences—while in New York City at *Parabola*, a magazine devoted to the dissemination and exploration of materials relating to the myths, symbols, rituals, and art of earth's religious and cultural traditions.

Through Faisu Mukunana's engaging, heart-felt stories, he has become intrigued by Taiwan—its friendly, hard-working people, and their lives and traditions—and hopes someday to visit the proud nation. Mr. Smith lives in Holmdel, New Jersey, with his wife, a professional figure skater; they have a son, a former wildland firefighter now teaching and living in Harlem, New York.

Aboriginal Population Distribution

(This map shows the fourteen major tribes of Taiwan. The Tsou tribe is concentrated in the Alishan Range, a mountainous area in Taiwan's central-southern region.)

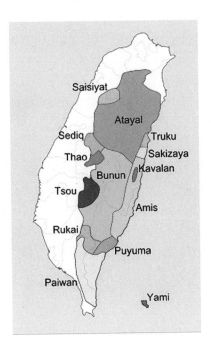

(Source: *https://en.wikipedia.org/wiki/Taiwanese_indigenous_peoples 2020*)

My Dear Ak'i,
Please Don't Be Upset

Author: Faisu Mukunana
Publisher: Taiwan Indigenous Voice
Serenity International
Translator: Yao-Chung Tsao
Editor: Cort Smith
Designer: Chung Pei-Yin
Executive Editors: C. J. Anderson-Wu, Lin Yi-Miao, Liu Ya-Mei
Cover Image: Yao-Chung Tsao
Cover Price: US $15, CAD $18, NTD 380
ISBN: 978-986-6245-05-3
Date of Publication: January 2021

The publication of this book is made possible
in part by the grant from Taiwan's National Culture and Arts Foundation

 國家文化藝術基金會
National Culture and Arts Foundation
NCAF